PHILOSOPHICAL RHETORIC

PHILOSOPHICAL RHETORIC

The function of indirection in philosophical writing

Jeff Mason

ROUTLEDGE
London and New York

First published in 1989 by Routledge
11 New Fetter Lane, London EC4P 4EE
29 West 35th Street, New York, NY 10001

© 1989 Jeff Mason

Data conversion by Columns of Reading
Printed in Great Britain by
Biddles Ltd, Guildford and Kings Lynn

British Library Cataloguing in Publication Data

Mason, Jeff, 1945–
Philosophical rhetoric: the function
of indirection in philosophical writing.
1. Philosophy
I. Title
100

ISBN 0–415–03043–9
ISBN 0–415–03044–7 Pbk

Library of Congress Cataloging in Publication Data

Mason, Jeff, 1945-
Philosophical rhetoric.
Bibliography: p.
Includes index.
1. Philosophy–Authorship. 2. Rhetoric–Philosophy.
3. Methodology. I. Title.
B52.7.M38 1989 808′0661 88–32194
ISBN 0–415–03043–9
ISBN 0–415–03044–7 (pbk.)

For their long and loving support I dedicate this book to my parents, Bernard and Elsie Mason.

CONTENTS

ACKNOWLEDGMENTS

I want to thank my teachers, my colleagues at Middlesex Polytechnic, and the University of California at Irvine where Professor Gerasimos Santas and the members of the philosophy department made me feel most welcome during my sabbatical leave, 1986–7.

Among my teachers I'd like to mention those who have left an indelible mark on my own philosphical development: J.B. Close, Marvin Shagam, Helen Heise, William Macomber, Lloyd Reinhardt, and David Hamlyn; among my colleagues: Jonathan Rée, Doreen Maitre, David Conway, Peter Washington, and Claud Pehrson. My special thanks go to Middlesex Polytechnic for providing a good environment in which to learn and grow.

I must acknowledge my debt to French theoreticians, particularly Derrida, for waking me from my analytic slumbers. The reason I do not engage directly with the details of their discussions in my book is that they do it so much better themselves.

Finally, I want to thank my wife, Linda, for all the work she has done helping me to prepare the final draft of the book. It has been a labor of love.

PREFACE

This book is the first result of seven years' reflection on the relation between philosophy and literary theory. For a philosopher schooled in the discipline of analytic philosophy, but never properly disciplined, the experience has been exhilarating, frightening, and perplexing. For someone taught to value clarity and logical cogency, confrontation with the writings of such authors as Kierkegaard, Nietzsche, and Heidegger, Barthes, Foucault, Lacan, and Derrida among others, produced a bewildering array of problems.[1]

The question came up: why bother with the whole business? It is perfectly possible to pursue a philosophical career and pay virtually no attention to any of the writings I mentioned above. Many seem incomprehensible, foolish, obscure, or wrong-headed. According to this narrative, the arguments, such as they are, can be shown to be unsound by the quick revelation of fallacious reasoning. It is perfectly feasible to remain philosophically unperturbed by the writings of continental hotheads.

I was amazed by this continental divide: Anglo-American analytic philosophy on one side, continental on the other. Hold up a page from Quine's *Word and Object*.[2] Now hold up a page of Derrida's *Margins of Philosophy*.[3] If both are philosophical writings, then they are of very different kinds. What is the difference? We must look to particular writings to work out the answer in any detail, but overall the conclusion I reach is that the difference lies in what I call *philosophical rhetoric*.

This work is the outline of a way to think of philosophy, rhetoric, and poetry, or to think philosophy/rhetoric-poetry together. The concept of philosophical rhetoric is meant to bridge the gap between the two without attempting to close it. It is the attempt to think philosophy and rhetoric together. However, it is important to be clear that this is not a work in literary theory. The goal is not simply to examine philosophical writings as literature, though that is part of it, but to locate them in a context which transcends philosophy, narrowly conceived. Philosophical writings are produced in particular social and historical settings. They are interventions in a rhetorical field of unexpressed assumptions and beliefs.

Philosophy is written for an audience and its main point is to bring this audience around to the way of thinking and looking at the world advocated by the text. To bring this about the writing aims to persuade the audience of the truth of its central claims. It is idle to suppose that philosophical writing is free of persuasive force, that it consists of logical argument alone. Philosophical arguments, their premises, conclusions, and the logic connecting them, are in fact part of the overall persuasive force of philosophical writings.

In order to forge the concept of philosophical rhetoric, I examine samples of philosophical writings from a wide spectrum of authors and styles of writing. However, instead of examining particular arguments in a straightforward philosophical way, I look at them from the point of view of their effects upon audiences, whether or not the author intentionally aims to produce those effects.

To help me in this endeavor I have turned to the writings of J.L. Austin on the uses of language.[4] In particular, I develop the concept of the *perlocutionary act* as a way to understand the nature of philosophical persuasion. I distinguish between an illocutionary argument and a perlocutionary one. Perlocutionary arguments are at the heart of philosophical rhetoric. They utilize the devices or techniques of indirection and, if successful, promote specific effects in the audience. The nature of a perlocutionary argument in philosophical writings will become clearer in the course of the work.

The thesis I argue is that philosophical writings display a perlocutionary dimension which we ignore at the peril of failing to grasp the nature of philosophical writings and their production by writers and readers. My aim is to contribute to a wider understanding of the effects produced by philosophical writings and the means of achieving those effects. The overall tendency of many philosophical writings, and particularly the writings of the analytic philosophers, is to ignore their own rhetorical or poetic aspects. There is the presumption that philosophy can do without those rhetorical tricks and poetic tropes that bedevil non-philosophical discourse and make it unacceptable as a vehicle of truth.

On the contrary, if rhetoric and tropical language invalidate the quest for truth, then philosophical writing is also invalidated. The social and historical context of the production of philosophical writings ensures that a rhetoric-free philosophical investigation is not possible within the world as presently constituted. A world which supports philosophical writing but makes no use of rhetoric and poetic tropes may be conceivable, but it would be such a different world that philosophical writings as we find them in the texts of the discipline would no longer exist. Failing a radical restructuring of human existence, philosophical writings will continue perforce to use rhetorical and poetic devices to attempt to produce conviction in an audience.

The key to philosophical rhetoric lies in the techniques of indirection which pervade philosophical writings. Some authors make more use of such techniques than others, but all make some use of them. The techniques of indirection in philosophy have to do with what is indicated by the text but not spelled out or made explicit in it. We see indirection at work most clearly in the writings of philosophers such as Kierkegaard and Nietzsche, but as I will show, we also find it in such hard-headed authors as A.J. Ayer.[5] One difference is simply the extent to which indirect techniques are used in their philosophical writings. Another is the purpose to which indirection is put.

My aim is to preserve philosophy as a discipline of argument and logic, and at the same time to increase awareness of the ubiquity of rhetoric and poetic tropes in philosophical writing. I argue that the attempt to arrive at truth in philosophy is a legitimate one which is not incompatible with rhetoric. In fact, the distinguishing mark of philosophical rhetoric is precisely that it is used in the service of that very truth which is the subject of strict philosophical arguments. Those arguments themselves are part of a means of rational persuasion to the truth which is the hallmark of philosophical writings.

In what follows I allow the positions under review to speak for themselves. I go with the rhetoric of the various writings under investigation. Readers are not to expect that my own views are always the ones expressed. The book is full of different voices all clamoring to make themselves heard. My hope is that it will not be too difficult to tell the difference between what the "characters" say and what my own views are.

I am indebted to Hegel's *Phenomenology* in this approach.[6] On the one hand, there are the various voices which speak for themselves. On the other hand, we listen to the conflicting voices and take a vantage point outside the immediate polemical context in which the disputes occur. Thus we, who are listening in, will be in a position through memory and self-reflection to grasp what is at stake in the various philosophical rhetorics which sketch themselves out before us.

One difference between this work and Hegel's *Phenomenology* is that the current author has no overriding conception of totality which somehow resolves all outstanding difficulties. Nevertheless, the concept of philosophical rhetoric is a dialectical one in the weak sense that philosophy and rhetoric play off one another and generate those tensions between them which lead to a movement of thought. This movement aims toward truth conceived as an ideal terminus of philosophical reflection. Truth is the motor which drives philosophical investigation. It is more like one of Kant's regulative principles[7] than the Absolute Idea of Hegel's *Phenomenology*.

Another focus of the investigation is the status of tropical language in philosophical writings. The tropical resources of language provide one of the main supports of philosophical indirection. Metaphors, in particular, provide an inexhaustible supply of suggestive material for philosophical analysis and development. By inviting interpretation and appraisal, metaphors are instrumental to the development and recognition of different lines of philosophical investigation. Irony and paradox provide indirect means for producing in the audience a heightened and distanced self-consciousness. Such is Plato's technique for encouraging self-reflection and self-knowledge in the audience. Of course, neither Plato nor any other philosopher can force the audience to think in a certain way. At best the audience can be persuaded to go along or give assent. At worst the audience will be persuaded neither to believe nor to entertain the arguments of the philosopher. Plato's writing can as easily produce hostility or indifference in an audience as it can a love of philosophy.

Tropes, such as metaphor and analogy, provide the beginning points for philosophical investigation. They conjure up the "matter" of philosophy through sheer imagination and ingenuity. They open up the places of philosophical argument for development. They serve up an invitation to the audience to respond in some way. In particular, the audience is invited to orientate himself or herself in a certain way to the argument presented. The immediacy and concreteness of philosophical metaphors, analogies, and images make them memorable collection points for philosophical reflection, a place to begin.

The first hurdle is cleared after the audience has been successfully inducted into the philosophical project of the writing. The audience is at least prepared to put some effort into reading the text. Perhaps the single most important function of tropical writing is to put the audience in the right frame of mind to consider the work at hand.

There is a distinction between the overt and the covert philosophical rhetoric of the text. How a text is taken is not wholly determined by the dominant line of persuasive force. We will detect cross-rhetorics at work which disrupt the smooth flow of the official line. The effects produced by a philosophical text depend as much on the attitude of the audience as on the text which is read. That is why and how authors lose control of their own productions the moment they become public possessions. An author or writing can do no more than indicate or point to the stance to be taken up by the audience. Tropical language in philosophical writing provides the most efficient and concentrated way to serve the perlocutionary argument of the text. We must look to specific writings for examples.

The study as a whole is meant to draw out a hitherto neglected feature of the philosophical landscape. It invites us to look at philosophical writing in a way which does not immediately land us in the thicket of internal philosophical debates. It bids us be aware of the indirect techniques of philosophical persuasion which are at work in philosophical writings. How persuasive it is, I will leave to the reader to decide.

Chapter One

INTRODUCTION: PHILOSOPHY AND RHETORIC

The themes of this book will surprise those who expect a work of philosophy to address itself directly to the question of the truth or falsity of "philosophical theses". To such readers what follows will not appear to be philosophy at all. Of course, it all depends upon what one takes philosophy to be.

According to one fairly common understanding of the task of philosophy, it is to address very general and abstract questions, arguing from premises to conclusions, analyzing basic concepts, and keeping the whole discussion free from the distractions, interruptions and digressions of non-philosophical by-play. The idea is to clarify and elucidate in straightforward fashion various positions in philosophy and then to anticipate and defend them from objections and criticisms.

It may be that the investigations in this book will have implications for some of the traditional debates in philosophy of mind and epistemology, perhaps even metaphysics. However, its aim will not be to address these issues directly. On the contrary, the writing of philosophy will be examined with an eye to what does not occur in argumentation, deduction, and defence. It will be concerned with what could be called "marginal" issues in philosophical writing; for example, the use of rhetorical and poetic tropes, indirect communication, persuasion, and philosophical ingenuity in devising and exploring the topics of philosophical discussion.

By taking this tack I do not mean to disparage the traditional approaches to the subject. In the ancient battle between poetry and philosophy, I do not wish to take sides with poetry against philosophy. This has already been done, and is being done, by

1

such figures as Derrida, Deleuze, and De Man, and in general by current movements of post-structuralist and post-modernist thought.[1] We find a parallel approach in the work of American philosophers such as Putnam, Goodman, and Rorty.

The criticisms leveled against traditional conceptions of philosophy can be summed up by Derrida's discussion of *logocentrism* in western thought. This attack considers the western project of philosophy to ascertain the truth of various matters to be tyrannical and oppressive. The expressed view that philosophy attempts to get to the truth is, on this account, nothing but a smoke-screen masking a will to power and domination. It is a drive for mastery and authority which disguises itself as the search for truth.

In the writings of Foucault we find the equation power = knowledge firmly expressed.[2] I agree that knowledge is tied to power, a power which finds its base in the institutions of contemporary life. Foucault makes this abundantly clear in his discussion of the birth of the clinic, the history and control of "madness," the "science" of penology, etc. A parallel case can be made in the marginal field of philosophy itself.

Philosophy, it can be argued, has its main mode of existence circumscribed by its institutional context. We can, perhaps, work out a history of education along the same lines as the history of prisons. We find a definite authority structure in the institutions of philosophy, a hierarchy of positions and opinions within academic settings. We find validating procedures for the grading and passing of generations of students according to set patterns. The question of whose knowledge is authoritative, especially in a field as amorphous as philosophy, is one which cannot be settled on the merits of argument alone. It often turns upon whose knowledge it is, what that person's qualifications are, what position he or she occupies, and so on.

As valuable as such an investigation might be in showing us how ideas and power structures interrelate, that is not my aim here. I do not wish to deconstruct the philosophical enterprise. That can be safely left to other, and more hostile, hands. On the contrary, there is room for people with inquiring and open minds to discuss the central issues of human life and capacities with an eye to the truth. We can, in fact, assess arguments, discuss them, and come to tentative agreements about them, though final conclusions may not be within our reach. Truth is an ideal which lies outside institutional and authoritative settings, but its discussion is carried on within them.

In what follows I am going to try to make sense, to make my remarks coherent and intelligible. In that way I suppose my writing can be labeled logocentric. If that is the case, I will not apologize for it. Nevertheless, there are certain things which the French thinkers write in their often obscure and confusing way which do have the ring (can I say it?) of truth. There is indeed more going on in philosophical texts than a straightforward account of argument and philosophical method will allow. What is not said is often crucial to our comprehension of what is said. What is going on around an argument can be more persuasive than the argument itself. There is rhetoric, even poetry, in philosophy, which often goes without comment. The aim of this book is not to condemn philosophy or philosophers but to raise philosophic consciousness of what is going on in the periphery of philosophical writing.

Of course this project may raise some hackles. Plato's ghost stalks all those who attempt a philosophical poetics or try to rehabilitate philosophical rhetoric. This again is part and parcel of the old quarrel between philosophy and poetry which Plato himself helped to start and which has yet to come to an end. My own position here is a dangerous one because I seek a middle ground, and we all know what happens to those who sit in the middle. They are likely to be shot at from both sides. Nevertheless, it would be well to begin by rehearsing the old argument briefly to see if a middle position is attainable.

Plato's criticism of poetry and rhetoric stems from his belief that the goal of philosophical inquiry is a truth which lies outside the uncertainties of human life and its vicissitudes. The world in which we live, for Plato, casts a veil upon truths which lie outside time and space, particularity, and chance circumstances. We catch a glimpse of this world in plane geometry, logic, and mathematics, where necessity and atemporality reign supreme. Hence, admission to the academy was contingent upon the learning of mathematics. The idea is that the study of necessary and a priori truths frees the mind from its dependence upon the body and its failings.

Plato's separation of the soul and the body is part of his strategy to attain knowledge of a supersensible world. Only by leaving the

3

body and the senses behind can the soul, by itself alone, contemplate the Forms of Being, which lie beyond the veil of appearances. The problem with both poetry and rhetoric is that they are impure and are not based on knowledge. The poets, Plato insists, are divinely inspired and therefore unable to give an account (*logos*) of their poetry. The rhetoricians, on the other hand, are so wrapped up in the uncertainties of life, so orientated toward success in the courts and the assemblies, that they give little thought to the truth of the matters of which they speak so eloquently. They are pedlars of probabilities, not certainties. They deal in the contingencies of life, not in the knowledge of pure Forms.

Plato's most stringent attack upon the rhetoricians and sophists takes place in the *Gorgias*. In that dialogue they are likened to panders who seek to please and convince but not to teach truth on the basis of knowledge. Plato notes that the philosopher is at a disadvantage here. He is in the position of the dietician arguing his case with a pastry cook before a jury of children.[3] What chance does he have in such circumstances?

The arguments of the philosophers are difficult, require concentration and attention, and make no concessions to the weaknesses of the audience. The rhetorician, on the other hand, is well aware of the weaknesses of his audience. He reads them like a book and tells them what he wants them to believe in a form which will be palatable to them. Hence the truth goes out the window, for unlike the possessors of specialist knowledge, the sophists and rhetoricians simply manipulate words for their own or their patron's ends.

This harsh attack is ameliorated in the *Phaedrus*, but skepticism with regard to the usual practices of sophists and rhetoricians persists. There is always a danger that in unscrupulous hands the techniques of rhetoric will degenerate into mere demagoguery. Skill in the use of the techniques of persuasion gives no guarantee that they will be used for good ends and true beliefs. Like the pastry cook, the rhetorician is the master of a knack learned from experience,[4] not the master of a true skill or art (*techne*).

This bald contrast between philosophy, which aims at the truth, and rhetoric, which aims merely to please and convince, points up a recurrent theme in this old quarrel, the distinction between substance and ornament. Philosophy aims at substance, rhetoric at mere ornamentation. Matters of dubious worth are "dressed up" in words, and words can cover a multitude of sins. Such a distinction persists in many quarters up to the present day. Metaphorical and, in general, tropical language has often been held to be mere dressing up of thought which adds nothing to its substance.

This criticism stands or falls with the philosophical project set up by Plato and other philosophers who follow his lead. If the aim is to express ahistorical truths in plain, unadorned prose, then skill in the use of words to express ideas is just so much froth to be discarded. Yet Plato is a poet. His philosphy is full of metaphors and rhetorical strategies and he used them very well. He created what are, perhaps, the three most famous of all philosophical metaphors, viz. the sun, the line, and the cave. These can be used to introduce, summarize, and unpack the main tenets of Plato's philosophy. It is perhaps why, in the teaching of Plato, book VII of the *Republic* captures so much attention.

Much has been made of Plato's use of irony, verbal play, jesting, and so on to set the stage for his positive views. Plato's Socrates, while being made to protest many times that he is only a plain speaker, is actually the master of all rhetorical techniques. He quotes the poets and praises Homer as often as he criticizes him. He engages in literary criticism with the best sophists of the land and is not above using verbal trickery to catch his interlocutors unawares.

Perhaps Plato's use of rhetoric has primarily a pedagogical function in the dialogues. Philosophy is a strange discipline, not readily accessible to unreflective human beings. Anyone who has taught introductory philosophy classes will recognize that one of the main tasks is to help students realize that there are philosophical problems in the first place. A common student reaction is simple incomprehension as to why anyone would bother to get involved in "philosophical" questions in the first place. They seem to lack relevance.

I have argued elsewhere[5] that Plato employs the technique of "estrangement" to induce people into the language-game of philosophy. In fact he "turns the world upside down" in order to do this. One of the reasons for Socrates' condemnation is his subversion of the old traditional Greek way of thought and life. This comes out clearly in the *Gorgias* in which Callicles[6], the Athenian man of action, condemns Socrates for staying away from the public life of the citizen and whispering instead to a few youths in a corner. Acting as a private person and thinking for himself, Socrates introduces whole generations into an inverted position which washes its hands of what is most crucial to the *polis*, namely, the running of the practical and uncertain affairs of life.

Plato's metaphors contribute to this job of estrangement. We can see this most clearly in the cave analogy in which suffering humanity is seen as chained beneath the ground, mistaking the shadows on the wall for reality.[7] The progress of someone liberated from those chains is a painful one. The break from uncriticized assumptions and beliefs must be forced. Finally, the initiate emerges from the cave only to be blinded by the light of the sun, which is reality. This liberation of the individual from unreflective, habitual life is also an alienation from the world of the senses and custom. To return to the cave is to suffer a reverse blindness of the kind one has upon entering a dark room on a bright afternoon. The philosopher has trouble finding his way about in the world of civil life. He cannot find his way to the courts or the assembly, and can easily fall prey to the machinations of ambitious people. Callicles warns Socrates that the philosopher is liable to be put to death for his unorthodox views and will be helpless to defend himself.

This is not to say that Plato cannot defend his views. He can and does. What it does mean is that Plato uses the most powerful metaphors he can deploy to help in what is essentially a rhetorical project of creating conviction. The conviction he wants to produce is that philosophy is worth while, and that the quest for truth is worth the trouble it undoubtedly brings with it. To this end Plato is not above employing the very techniques he condemns in others who are not, perhaps, on his moral plane. So the case against poetry and rhetoric is not so clear cut as it might seem at first.

Plato's emphasis on knowledge of the Forms shifts his whole discussion away from the "timely" (used here to mean "pertaining to the moment") issues which are at the basis of rhetorical activity. Unlike philosophy, which in his view aims at truths far beyond the dust and dirt of this world, rhetoric is at home precisely in this world of uncertainties. Aristotle notes this point in the *Rhetoric*[8] where he makes it plain that the rhetorician has to deal with a world of probability. As such it stands with ethics on the side of practical reason, opposed to theoretical reason which deals with the sciences.

In the *Ethics*[9] Aristotle remarks that doing the right thing, the virtuous thing, is not something that can be taught in the manner of the sciences. To be virtuous is to judge and act correctly in the changing circumstances of the world. It is to act on the basis of one's character in such a way that one does the right thing, in the right way, and at the right place and time. Such action takes discernment on the part of the agent. The right thing to do cannot be worked out a priori. Rather, one must see how principle and circumstances come together in the particular situation.

The case of rhetoric is similar to this. When the orator seeks to persuade a jury or an assembly that a certain verdict is to be reached, or a certain course of action is to be followed, he must marshal all the facts and principles relevant to the desired outcome. As Aristotle puts it, he must bring together all the available means of persuasion. Certainty in these matters is simply not available. Though logical argument has a role to play in the putting of a case, logic alone cannot settle the issue. It is not like mathematics or geometry in which proofs are available and the results hold necessarily and with unrestricted generality. This is not the case in situations in which the techniques of rhetoric are needed.

Rhetoric begins and ends in the realm of opinions. Alternative points of view, verdicts, courses of action, etc. are never ruled out by logic. What matters in rhetoric is the particular judgment and the decision which follows upon it. Alternatives are ruled out by choice, and they can be opened up to further consideration in the future. Therefore, the activity of persuasion never permanently ceases but simply comes to a halt for the time being in a decision which is reached.

Only if the demand for absolute certainty and timeless truth is made does rhetorical activity come off second best. In areas where differences of opinion remain after all discussion, and a final conclusion cannot be reached, rhetorical argument is all there is and no longer second best to something else. As we shall see, this fact has a crucial bearing on the role of rhetoric in philosophy itself.

One of the central claims of this work will be that rhetoric is never absent from philosophy. It is like a river in the desert which is sometimes above ground where all can see it, but at other times sinks beneath the ground and becomes invisible. At those times it

7

might seem that rhetoric has lost its connection with philosophy and that we can make a firm distinction between the two. The avowed aim of Plato's philosophy is to do just this, create a wedge between philosophy and rhetoric to the detriment of rhetoric. But we would do well to remember a remark by Brutus in Cicero's *De Oratore*:[10]

> Whereas the persons engaged in handling and pursuing and teaching the subjects that we are now investigating were designated by a single title (the whole study and practice of the liberal sciences being entitled philosophy), Socrates robbed them of this general designation, and in his discussions separated the science of wise thinking from that of elegant speaking. . . . This is the source from which has sprung the undoubtedly absurd and unprofitable and reprehensible severance between the tongue and the brain, leading to our having one set of professors to teach us to think and another to teach us to speak.

A brief look at the contemporary philosophy journals should be enough to convince anyone that professional philosophers, though they perhaps think very well, could often use some rhetorical help. (I do not exclude myself; my training too is in the school of thought, not expression.) In many cases the severance between content and style in philosophy is nearly complete. This does not mean that there are no philosophers who write felicitously, but if they do, it seems almost an afterthought.

One reason for this, I suspect, is the emphasis upon philosophy as a kind of science or conceptual analysis. Especially in times of advance in logic, mathematics, and the hard sciences, philosophers seem to move in that direction. The results show up in the advance of technical vocabulary and more and more specialized and esoteric fields of study. There is no doubt that contemporary philosophical works are, for the most part, inaccessible to the layman.

This is not a complaint. There is no reason why philosophy should be easily accessible to everyone. But its inaccessibility hides, I believe, the fact that philosophical tracts are nevertheless rhetorical exercises and have some sort of style, though perhaps not a very elegant one. The stance of much philosophical writing, a stance of anonymity, impartiality, and objectivity, is, after all, a stance. It supposes that a certain game of philosophy is being played, but the rules are never laid out. If they were, we should have the beginnings of a rhetoric of contemporary philosophy.

A question which arises is why a study of rhetoric in philosophy should be of philosophical interest. It is not clear that it is always of such interest. Most debates in contemporary philosophy within established and mainstream traditions are far from considering such questions. Instead, the debates turn upon points within those traditions and unselfconsciously seek to persuade the already converted to this or that view. I say the "already converted" to refer to those who already participate in the line of debate as a whole. The particular point of persuasion then turns not on the value of the tradition or general philosophical orientation, but upon particular points which are up for grabs within that tradition.

For example, if we consider the line of arguments developed by what has been called "ordinary language philosophy" or "conceptual analysis" we will find particular issues addressed, but not the validity of the whole line of argument. Usually there is some mention of major thinkers in the field, their theories or theses, and the question is about their clarity, conciseness, validity, or truth. The backdrop is almost always what someone has said and whether it makes sense. After this, perhaps, the current speaker or writer will make his or her own contribution to the debate. The very notion of a "contribution" is telling. We contribute to something which is already in existence, something which is continuing, and something which, it is believed, is going somewhere.

This fact can give us a key to the observation that the rhetorical qualities of philosophical debate are for the most part ignored. Philosophers who contribute to a continuing debate do not need to convince others following the same path that that is the path to follow. A kind of rhetorical stasis sets in which reflects either a common agreement about what philosophy is and how it is to be done or a settled disposition not to raise these questions. When such agreement holds, the river of rhetoric sinks beneath the sands and gives the illusion that it is not there at all.

It is not always like this. In particular it is not like this at the present moment in philosophy. Whatever consensus may have existed, if it ever did, about what philosophy is and how it is to be pursued no longer obtains. It has become hard to speak about mainstream philosophy. Instead there are many streams, and to exclude any one of them in favor of another is to ignore the ferment in philosophy.

This ferment has a number of causes. One of the most important is the development of interdisciplinary studies of many descriptions. Philosophy borders many branches of learning, from anthropology to linguistics, from science to politics, from literature to history, from medicine to technology, from business to feminism. Another factor is the emergence of continental philosophy into higher visibility in the world of so-called "Anglo-American" philosophy, and the higher visibility of "Anglo-American" philosophy on the continent. On the one hand, we have the continental invaders advancing under the banners of Marxism, existentialism, phenomenology, hermeneutics, structuralism, post-structuralism, deconstruction, and post-modernist thought. Going the other way we find conceptual analysis, speech-act theory, and the preoccupation with language so ably developed by British and American philosophers.

Relations between different philosophical interest groups may not always be very cordial, but there is real ferment. There are a growing number of games in town, and to get a hearing each must practice a stronger form of rhetoric. I will show that this is the case both for the present period of philosophical development and for past periods as well.

It is a commonplace of ancient rhetoric that persuasive techniques are needed in uncertain situations. In classical rhetoric the uncertain situations in question were those of the court and the assembly, judicial and deliberative rhetoric. We cannot, for the most part, deductively prove our case in court or the assembly. The ancient sophists who first studied these matters were looking for clues which tell us something of the art of effective speaking. There were good speakers long before anyone ever thought of devising a manual on the art of speaking. It is plausible that observers noticed that various speakers gave a particularly good account of themselves and found success in the court and assembly. The question then was why they were so good, i.e. successful.

Observation led to hypotheses about what they did that was so effective. We can look to any number of manuals of rhetoric over the centuries to see what emerged from this study. Certain features of effective speaking were abstracted and codified. I do not wish to reproduce such a manual here, but it would be well to summarize the outline of such studies.

In Hellenistic times manuals of rhetoric were divided into five parts. The first dealt with finding what to say and was titled *inventio*. Then came the arrangement of the material called *dispositio*; the finding of appropriate verbal formulations, *elocutio*; the means of memorizing the speech, *memoria*; and the actual delivery, *pronunciatio*.

In order to be an effective speaker, it is first necessary to have something to say and then to say it well. Saying it well has to do with the arranging of the parts of what is said into a whole and then with its delivery in speech. It is important to realize the importance of the connection between rhetoric and speech. Originally, rhetoric was tied to the existence of an oral culture which relied heavily upon verbal memory to collect and pass down the knowledge and traditions of a people. Rhetoric as a study arose only after the invention of writing, and henceforth slowly detached itself from speech and increasingly allied itself to writing. Nevertheless, for centuries the art of actually speaking to an audience remained very important, and for that reason a consideration of delivery remained a subject of rhetoric.[11]

However, it is not delivery which has received the major portion of attention but the other two parts, known in Latin as the *res* and the *verba*, the matter and the style. It was noticed that in order to speak and, later, to write well, it is necessary to develop arguments, recognize various kinds of appeals to an audience, notice fallacies, and so on. Then it is necessary to arrange this material in the most effective way. And finally there is the question of style, the identification of various schemes and tropes used in effective speaking.

Most important from the point of view of the present work are the questions of invention (*ingenium*) and topic (*topos*) or place of argument, and further of tropical language, particularly metaphor.

In classical accounts of rhetoric the topics (*topoi*) have to do with finding something to say, with finding places of argument. Students of rhetoric, it was hoped, would be able to find something to say about almost any question by familiarizing themselves with various topics of argument. The topics themselves were divided into two: the general topics and the special topics. The general topics were held to apply to all sorts of subjects and comprised such commonplaces as definition, comparison, relationship, circumstances, and testimony. The special topics, as the name suggests, were particular places of argument suitable to more restricted discussions. The more "special" a topic became the more it involved specialized knowledge, and the further it moved from the general techniques of rhetoric.

Now my questions is whether there are things that could be called philosophical *topoi*. The answer seems to be plainly "yes." However, though philosophers use the general *topoi* of the rhetoricians without thinking about them, and indeed invented many of them, that is not the sense I wish to stress here. Rather, I have in mind the philosophical topics which we will find in any philosophy curriculum. Some of them, such as definition, cause and effect, and logic, which are general topics in rhetoric, are special topics in philosophy. The rhetorician does not so much question as use them. A brief survey or list will be sufficient to point out some of the many philosophical topics to be found in the literature.

Topics: mind and body, machine intelligence, dialectic/anti-dialectic, free will and determinism, ontology, epistemology, logic, ethics, political philosophy, aesthetics, induction, philosophy of science, realism/non-realism, fact/value, counter-factuals, possible worlds, space and time; language, sense, meaning, intention, truth values, assertability conditions; signifier/signified, *différance*, the unconscious, spatiality/temporality, structure, synchrony/diachrony, "spatial" history; causality, explanation, interpretation, deconstruction, etc.; Heraclitus, Parmenides, Socrates, Aristotle, Aquinas, Descartes, Kant, Hegel, Marx, Nietzsche, Freud, Lacan. Frege, Russell, Carnap, Wittgenstein, Austin, Quine, etc.

Anyone who has studied philosophy formally should be able to take up a position on some of these topics. What positions and topics are available will be largely determined by institutional structures. Both the teaching and learning of philosophy are governed by rules and regulations for the granting and taking of degrees in colleges and universities. Both have institutionalized constraints put upon the curriculum which restrict the availability of topics covered.

There is nothing really sinister about this restriction. It is a practical requirement. Imagine trying to have something significant to say about everything in the long list of topics above. There are so many different things about which so much has already been said that it is very difficult to approach philosophy without some kind of pre-selection of texts, languages, and philosophers. The curricula of universities and colleges around the world are just this, a pre-selection of texts and conditions for the running and passing of courses.

A philosophical topic must first pass muster in its own institution before it can be included in the curriculum. For example, in the nineteenth century there was debate in England about whether to include Hegel on the syllabus of British universities.[12] The answer was "no." It was felt that though Hegel had something to say which is, perhaps, philosophically interesting, it was not a fit subject for the English undergraduate. How topics come to be included in the curricula of universities is an interesting historical question but is not the point at issue here. The point is that to do philosophy involves taking one's place in discussions which have already evolved and having something to say about them.

There is a close connection between what philosophy is considered to be and the given curriculum of a philosophy department. Part of the rhetoric of philosophy itself has to do with choosing what will pass as fit topics for philosophical teaching and learning. Anyone who has participated in the formation of courses, curriculum development, etc., will be aware of the wide opportunity for disagreement open to the participants. This is one point where the rhetoric of philosophy comes into its own. It is necessary to persuade one's colleagues that such and such a text or figure should or should not be included in planned revisions to the curriculum. The outcome, as in the case of the exclusion of Hegel from undergraduate studies in England, can affect the course of philosophical development.

It would be idle to pretend that such discussions are carried on purely in the spirit of disinterested objectivity. There are many axes to be ground in the formation of syllabuses, many interests to be served or slighted, many strong views to be put forward. It is generally necessary to marshal all the available means of persuasion if space is to be created for a new philosophical topic.

In the contemporary scene we need look no further than the new topics which have slowly carved themselves a place in our institutions of higher education. I am thinking particularly of such topics as medical and business ethics, feminism, artificial intelligence, and so on. Twenty years ago such topics were not thought of, let alone argued for. Particularly in the Anglo-American situation with which I am most familiar, the "mainstream" occupied a seemingly unassailable high ground. One could guess, simply on the basis of considering the English-speaking philosophical world, what the topics considered would be. We would expect a prominent place to be given to logic, epistemology, metaphysics (logical ontology), philosophy of language and mind; also philosophy of politics, ethics, and perhaps aesthetics. We could expect that the representative figures would be found in the tradition of empiricism and perhaps Kantianism, with special emphasis upon the line descending from Frege through Russell to Wittgenstein. We could expect the dominant tenor of a philosophy department to be that of philosophical analysis or "ordinary language" philosophy.

In the last twenty years, however, the philosophical world in the Anglo-American sphere has seen a number of changes. The hegemony of "analytic" philosophy has been challenged on a number of fronts, and successfully, too. This has been the result, in part, of a rhetorical assault upon the old preoccupations of professional philosophers.

As I mentioned before, a rhetorical stasis is achieved when participants in the tradition agree about the game they are playing and the rules of the game. There is no need for a visible rhetoric under such conditions. One of the reasons for the successful introduction of the new topics into philosophy is the inadequate rhetorical defences of the old. The "analytic" philosophers had no explicit rhetorical legs to stand on, as it were, and lost ground by default. Many new topics which first met with blank indifference, amused condescension, incomprehension, or stiff-backed hostility, have now taken their place on the philosophical agenda.

Another feature of nearly all the new topics or places which have been introduced into philosophy is their proximity to other disciplines. Consider medical ethics. The advent of the new health technology – the ability to prolong life beyond anything that has ever been known in history, the ease of abortion, the development of techniques to increase fertility, test-tube babies, etc. – has sharpened a number of ethical questions which demand immediate consideration and a practical outcome.

"Ethics" as the domain of hermetically sealed philosophical investigation is no longer seen as self-sufficient and self-justifying. The demand for ethical study to be "relevant" to "hot" contemporary problems has led to the development of courses suited to this new concern. Some may claim that strictly speaking only the older, more purely theoretical concerns of "mainstream" ethics deal with "philosophical" ethical problems, and that the new topics show an uncomfortable and impure mixture of empirical studies, personal commitments, and subjective bias. However, this criticism must be seen against the background of a certain conception of what philosophical ethics is or must be. The objection is itself rhetorical and takes its place in a rhetorical philosophical field in which the new concerns, for a number of reasons, are making themselves persuasive to a growing number of specialists and students alike.

Some of these reasons are not really theoretical at all. It should be noted that philosophy as a professional and teaching discipline is on the defensive at the moment in a way which makes new approaches necessary. We find, therefore, at various levels, the "selling" of philosophy. No longer able to keep its aloof status, people interested in keeping institutional philosophy alive must mount a public relations campaign of no small proportions. Needless to say, no one is going to come out and put it this way, but that does not prevent it from happening. Nearly all the new topics find a constituency to work for. In medical ethics, for example, we find philosophers taking up employment teaching service courses for doctors, nurses, and health professionals. The same holds true for business ethics, where philosophy courses find· a place in business curricula.

Perhaps the largest growth area in philosophy surrounds the "new" topic of critical thinking. As I see it, critical thinking is an umbrella term which covers a rhetorical strategy for not just philosophers but also other hard-pressed humanities teachers to come to grips with the changing world of intellectual fashion in the academic and non-academic world. Fewer students opt for a humanities education because it is seen, rightly or wrongly, as irrelevant to more practical goals of life. Other fields, therefore, are reaping increasing numbers of students. Nevertheless, the old idea of a "liberal education" is not dead, and finds its avatar in the idea of critical thinking.

There is, as I see it, a certain practical rhetorical strategy behind the current interest in critical thinking. Behind it is a desire to conserve and increase the job prospects for philosophers and other humanities professionals. This might seem like a mundane concern hardly fitted to the dignity of philosophy or other humanities subjects. However, appearances are deceptive. It is not exceptional for extramural considerations to impinge upon deliberations which appear on the surface to be of merely academic interest.

Philosophy is hardly unique. While its language is often severe and purportedly neutral and analytic, its practitioners are human beings with many interests to promote, including their own interests in teaching and research. But the existence of the academic world which supports this teaching and research is an uncertain one. The colleges and universities are human institutions, built by people, maintained by them, and financed by them. As such their future is uncertain and the arena in which they are maintained, directed, and financed is a rhetorical one.

In the context of scarce resources, unemployment, and a conservative political climate, the humanities have to be justified before the public. The "critical thinking" movement is one such justification. The case is argued that students in this complicated world need to know more than the limited special expertise in which they are trained. A proper education, it is maintained, should be well rounded, should make students fit to be citizens of a democracy facing many daunting and complex issues. Students should be aware of the history of their culture and the other cultures of the world. They should be able to grasp, at least in outline, the cultural achievements which inform their society, and they should be able to take a wider and longer view of their situation than concentration on a limited field of study can supply. To be able to think critically is part of this education.

These may be good arguments. However, this does not mean that they are not part of a rhetorical strategy to convince the relevant bodies that the learning of the humanities, and philosophy in particular, has a place in the future of education in our colleges and universities.

It is a mistake to try to make a hard distinction between "pure" philosophy and philosophy as a set of social practices and institutions. It is as much a mistake as trying to make a similar distinction between philosophy and rhetoric itself. The relationship of the philosopher, as a professional, to philosophy will always be rhetorical to the extent that he or she is bound up with wider social enterprises through the institutionalized practices of the discipline.

Anyone who has ever taught philosophy in the setting of an institution will realize that a "place" or a "space" in which to talk philosophy is hard to find. Within the complicated networks of time-tables, committee meetings, curriculum planning, political maneuvers, and so on, room must be made to sit down quietly, without the distraction of preoccupations from the mundane world, to think about a philosophical question, problem, or topic.

When ostensibly academic discussions are raised in committee and planning meetings, they are raised, not for their own sakes alone, but for their ideological bearing on the matters in hand. Sometimes such meetings can have a radical effect on those whose interests hang on their outcome. This is a rhetorical arena in whch the marshalling of opinion is crucial. In it, philosophical argument is inescapably rhetorical. We cannot do anything better here than to seek to persuade.

There are a number of ways in which this can be interpreted. On a cynical interpretation, the function of committees is simply to allow the free play of competitive egos and the quest of mastery. All the allusions to high-flown philosophical theories, the quest for truth, the ideals of education, and so on, are nothing but artful ruses. And besides, if philosophers in committee meetings get too embroiled in philosophical debate, they are likely to be drawn up short for wasting time.

To illustrate with an example drawn from my own experience, there seem to be at least two possible conceptions of how philosophy should be taught, each of which radically excludes the other. The one might be called "topical," the other "historical." The topical view assumes that philosophy is the attempt to come to grips with certain questions and problems which are of current interest. The history of the subject is only of relevance when it has a direct bearing on the questions or problems currently exercising and exciting philosophical work. On the other hand, the historical view holds that philosophy, in many respects, is just the history of philosophy itself, of what philosophers have said. It is impossible to grasp the topics of current philosophical interest without

understanding something of their historical antecedents. Furthermore, it might be added that there is more in philosophy than what
is of current interest.

The path one chooses has a radical effect upon curriculum
development. To go one way sets us a syllabus of more or less
static topics surrounded by reading lists. (Some of the reading, no
doubt, will be snippets of the writings of historical philosophers.)
We would find, at least in the Anglo-American setting, which is by
and large topic-orientated, such things as philosophy of language,
mind, metaphysics, logic, epistemology; the problem of induction,
scientific method, ethics, aesthetics, politics. The point is that we
would look for the enduring "problems of philosophy" and
structure our teaching around them. There might perhaps be one
or two historical survey courses just to round off the syllabus.

To go the other way results in a very different syllabus. Here we
would find offered for study a series of authors from different
historical periods. They would be offered as complete thinkers in
their own right, and not merely contributors to a current debate.
Their philosophy would be understood in the light of the wider
historical circumstances of the day, and the attempt would be
made to come to some overall view of the authors' work. The topics
which form the backbone of the other course figure here as themes
developed in an author's work. Thus, whereas Hume's work might
be cited in a discussion of the problem of causation in a topic
centred approach, the topic of causation would come up in a
discussion of Hume's philosophy in the historical approach.

There are pros and cons to each side in this debate. Taking the
side of the topic- or problem-centred approach, we might argue in
the following way. Studying what philosophers said in the past and
trying to get their theories right is all well and good. But the point
of philosophical argument is to reach the truth about questions
which we ask right now. Interpretative skills alone will not bring us
closer to our goal. It does not matter what these philosophers said
so much as whether what they said is true. It could very well be
that an investigation of what historical philosophers have said is
instructive in the kinds of mistakes it is possible to make, but this is
a merely negative result of looking at the history of the subject. It
cannot take the place of developing the theoretical skills necessary
to handle these questions in their own right.

Taking the other side, we might argue that learning philosophical techniques is all well and good, but what matters is an understanding of the context in which such techniques are used. This context can only be historical. Furthermore, the topics, questions, and problems which the topic-centred approach naïvely accepts as its beginning points have themselves a long history. Some have changed beyond recognition. Some have remained basically the same, but are now used in different contexts. We need whatever aids we can find to help us with our current problems, and there is no reason not to use the accumulated thoughts of philosophical history to help us.

I have presented this rhetorical confrontation in bald terms. Further criticism can undoubtedly be made against both approaches, and perhaps a synthesis is possible. The discussion can go on and on. My point is only that the end of the discussion is a decision, not the conclusion of a deductive argument. This does not mean that the results of the decision are any less crucial for different ways of doing philosophy. The fact that there is always something more to be said, and not enough time to explore every avenue, means that the end of the discussion is always pre-emptive. The result is an action that is at the same time a philosophical action, bringing with it a whole approach to the subject and its teaching. Once this has been agreed, the scope of rhetorical activity contracts to a certain extent, since now only adjustments to an already established framework remain to be decided.

Even where the general outlines are agreed, however, there are still many opportunities for the use of rhetorical strategies. For instance, different views often arise over the fine tuning of a syllabus, and as there is little chance to settle on the right adjustment by any kind of agreed method, we are still left with the forces of persuasion to bring about cooperation and some kind of consensus.

What has been said here about two differing conceptions of philosophy and how they should be taught also holds true with respect to the introduction of new topics into syllabuses. All that can be mustered are "probable" arguments, not in the sense of probabilities of fact, but in the sense of probabilities of opinions on the matter at hand. That is not to say that individuals will not feel very strongly about some issues, and feel "certain" of various things; but this translates merely into "convictions" and not directly into truth. Whether it translates indirectly into truth is

19

another matter and one we shall leave undecided for the moment.

It is very difficult in this situation to get away from all bias, or even to know what "getting away from bias" might amount to. All we can do is work with the available means of persuasion to make our own case for the syllabus we prefer and try to show that it is the best course to take. To do this, of course, we must argue our case as best we can. And strictly philosophical arguments will be among those which count in discussions about philosophy syllabuses. My point is that these arguments will have force, will be persuasive, only if they are backed up by agreement on the "commonplaces" of a certain philosophical perspective. Agreement on these is what gives force to particular arguments. Disagreements here open the whole field of discussion to novel arguments and topics. It can also lead to an end of all discussion; the end of dialogue or communication; the end of philosophical talk as open-minded, cooperative investigation of some matter in order to get at its "truth."

A good example of this exists in the so-called "gulf" which separates "Anglo-American" from continental philosophy. One common story of this development traces the estrangement of the two traditions to the split between rationalism on the continent and empiricism in England, the preoccupation with intellect played off against the preoccupation with sense. The rupture, however, only became full blown, so this story goes, in the aftermath of Kant's transcendental idealism. The continentals, with some notable exceptions, went the way of absolute idealism and totalizing thought. The English stayed with empiricism after flirting with idealism, and the Americans developed pragmatism. In England the appearance of logical empiricism maintained itself through days of idealist optimism, and finally prevailed after the collapse of morale resulting from the First World War.

This is a speculative history of philosophy, but the fact remains that dialogue between the different worlds of philosophy largely ceased. There is a gaping lack of mutual understanding between Anglo-American and continental philosophy. This is because what is a commonplace on one side of the Channel is an absurdity or worse on the other side. There is no agreement upon the nature of philosophical activity or the appropriate language to use in discussing philosophical problems. If a kind of rhetorical stasis is maintained within the different schools of philosophy, between them is a rhetorical abyss. What is persuasive or convincing in a particular debate fails utterly when transplanted to the field of another.

However, the schools of philosophy are not where we must first turn to see the workings of philosophical rhetoric more clearly. Not all philosophers fit nicely into any school of thought. Some begin and end as outsiders in philosophical debates. In the next chapter we shall examine four such philosophers and use them as case studies in our investigation of indirection in philosophical writing.

Chapter Two

CASE STUDIES: SCHOPENHAUER, KIERKEGAARD, WITTGENSTEIN, AND NIETZSCHE

The philosophers in this chapter have one thing in common. They resist the temptation to absolutize reason. Schopenhauer does so in the name of Kant's transcendental idealism, Kierkegaard in the name of faith, Nietzsche of imagination, and Wittgenstein of multiplicity. The first three confront and react to the spectacle of Hegel's Absolute Spirit, and the last, to a form of logical atomism. Other than this resistance to the blandishments of reason, they also have aims in common which outstrip the resources of simple argument alone. It will be instructive to look at them as rhetorical philosophers *par excellence*. One point which will be examined in some detail is their status as outsiders in the philosophical world, philosophers who are read from time to time but never figure to a large extent in standard syllabuses. They seem to be tangential and isolated figures. As I hope to show, the fact that they all rely heavily upon rhetorical strategies to accomplish their effects has a close connection with their being loners on the philosophical scene. The case of Wittgenstein is complicated by the fact that a concerted effort has been made to incorporate him into a standard approach to philosophy. We will see how well this project has succeeded.

Let us begin with Schopenhauer. Schopenhauer insists that our knowledge is restricted to the world as it can be represented to our limited understanding and received by our limited senses. He is a Kantian and holds fast to the distinction between phenomenon and noumenon. Empirical knowledge is restricted to appearances. The subject knows an object which appears already conditioned. But to appear at all, the object must be conceived of as distinct from the subject which knows it. We are not talking about empirical knowledge if we assert the identity of subject and object in it. Standing in a cognitive relation to a thing restricts both things and knowers to distinct categories of being.

Schopenhauer bit the bullet and came out to identify the noumenon with will. Being-in-itself is will. Schopenhauer has trouble saying how he knows this, given his own strictures. Nevertheless, he gives a persuasive portrayal of a world perspective in which the abnegation of will is essential to overcome the dichotomy of subject and object and achieve the true death.[1]

It is interesting that Schopenhauer's works are filled with literary allusions, scatterings of sayings in a number of different languages, and liberal use of tropes. Regardless of the logical validity of some of his arguments and presuppositions, including those concerning the truth of transcendental idealism, Schopenhauer is an effective philosophical writer.

I want to turn the usual procedure around. Instead of asking what is wrong with Schopenhauer's philosophy in terms of weak or bad arguments, let us ask about the role of philosophical argument in the production of the rhetorical effects that are part of Schopenhauer's over-all philosophical/rhetorical strategy. He is trying to persuade us to look at the world in his way, examine the evidence, consider our own lives, and judge whether or not he is right.

Schopenhauer has a strong vision of the world and brings all available means of persuasion to his side. Strict philosophical argumentation is one of the means, but far from the only one, available to persuade a mostly philosophical audience. And Schopenhauer is not writing only to professional philosophers. What he had to say was of more than merely academic interest. He had a philosophy of life and living. It may not have been the most optimistic philosophy, but at least it faced up to the question of what it means to be a human being, what it is to have wisdom, and what is the best sort of life to live and death to die.

To get the reader to share his vision, Schopenhauer must create it out of whole cloth before our very eyes. In that sense *The World as Will and Representation*[2] is a poem, and Schopenhauer is a poet. He is making something which must come to life before our eyes so that we too will share the "vision." This is not a wholly rational goal, since there is no purely discursive method of conveying it. But if we extend our notion of "rationality" to include the finding and exploring of ends or purposes, as well as the means to them, then to that extent it is up to the reader to supply the vision which animates Schopenhauer's philosophy, and that includes the working through of straight philosophical argument. The creation of philosophical "effects," changes in world view, attitude, etc., as outside the control of the text, and outside the control of the author. Yet such effects can nevertheless be accomplished through the adroit use of rhetorical and poetic techniques for philosophical ends, namely the attainment of truth on some matter of general application.

I am not saying that the author consciously sets out to use means of persuasion and then picks the proper tropes to do so, though this might happen. A sensitive author is reaching for the best way to state the truth as he or she sees it. The words come unbidden and include the tropes and figures which litter even the tidiest of philosophy texts. Schopenhauer gives us a ripe example. We could almost tell the tale of his philosophy through picking out his central metaphors or maxims.

Recall the blind giant carrying a stunted but seeing dwarf around on its shoulders;[3] the intellect-vizier supplying the wishes of its master, the sultan-will;[4] and the invulnerable fortress of solipsism.[5] There are many more, like so many links on a chain. They tie together the main themes which Schopenhauer develops. Pithy sayings, vivid images, clever remarks all have a tendency to stick in the mind long after the details of the strict philosophical arguments have been forgotten.

I hear someone say that it's a pity the argument is forgotten, but the emblems are remembered. Are these not merely rhetorical tricks to get someone to think the thing that is not? Are we to suppose that images and metaphors give us real understanding? If Schopenhauer relies on tricks like these, so much the worse for him.

This is a possible line of attack and one which finds proponents. But there is another way to look at it. What if truth in philosophy comes more as a growing conviction over time than as the conclusion to particular logical arguments? Such truths would be tied to recollection and memory, and had best be memorable. Schopenhauer arrived at his philosophy over years. By the same token it might take years for his philosophy to sink in and take effect. This "sinking in" and "taking effect" are made possible by

24

those images and sentences which accumulate meaning over time through reflection and recollection.

Perhaps Plato was correct to stress the educative power of poetry. The words of the poets in the minds of the young are like seeds which take root and can be dislodged later only with great difficulty. Hence, for Plato, it was very important which bits of poetry to allow into the minds of the young. The sayings, images, and metaphors of Schopenhauer are seeds which, taking root in the mind, mature with time and prove themselves in experience, not simply in theory.

Schopenhauer is trying to do something which cannot be accomplished by straightforward argument alone. He is forced to rely upon indirect means to create the effects which are part of "seeing" the point. He tells us himself:

> Only the poorest knowledge, abstract secondary knowledge, the concept, the mere shadow of knowledge proper, is unconditionally communicable. If perceptions were communicable, there would then be a communication worth the trouble; but in the end everyone must remain within his own skin and his own skull, and no man can help another. To enrich the concept from perception is the constant endeavor of poetry and philosophy.[6]

It is left to the reader to look where Schopenhauer points without having everything spelled out. The reader can follow the hints and suggestions which Schopenhauer bodies forth in metaphor and story. However, the only way in which indirect communication can take place is through the unforced cooperation of the reader.

Contrary to the premise of *The Godfather*, there is no such thing as an invitation which cannot be refused. Some invitations, it is true, are hard to refuse; but if one is ready to pay the penalty for non-compliance, any invitation can be refused. Schopenhauer's strategy is to bring about in the reader a "turning of the soul" in which everything which previously seemed dear now turns out to be the source of all our suffering. As he puts it at the end of *The World as Will and Representation*,[7] what to us may seem as nothing, to the truly wise seems a heaven, and what our ordinary attitudes tell us really matters, seems as nothing to the sage.

This reversal cannot be accomplished by main force. It is very hard to get someone who loves life to condemn it. Indirect means are called for. Persuasion is called for, a persuasion which calls to the whole person and not just to a part. Reason, for Schopenhauer, is impotent against the will. The best reason can do is present plausible pretexts to the will confirming its own desires. The will must be turned in its path, but at the same time made to think that it wants to go another way. We have here the cunning of reason which is not above subterfuge, beguilement, and seduction in the accomplishment of its end.

Why does Schopenhauer weary us with countless examples of the vanity of pride, ambition, avarice, and the rest? Why does he tell us what to expect in the stages on life's way? Why does he always remind us of the sufferings, disappointments, and disasters which accompany our lives? Because he wants to distance us from what we ordinarily do and think so that we might have the space in which to reflect on the likely outcome and ultimate meaning of all our unreflective activity.

Schopenhauer is a philosopher of the edge. He stands on the borders of the intelligible to make us consider the extremes of human life and thought. The result is that his philosophy may not be altogether coherent. There are fair criticisms to make of Schopenhauer's attempt to deal with Kant's noumenon. He does seem to be saying contradictory things at times, and also to be trying not to contradict himself. Nevertheless, if Schopenhauer is trying to get readers to change their whole way of looking at things, then "noumenal" contradictions may signal a breakdown of his argument at certain points, but do not, or need not, signal a breakdown of his whole project in philosophy, which is to bring about a change in the reader's outlook and attitudes. Doing this is what requires him to use indirect means of communication, and makes his philosophy intrinsically rhetorical or even poetic.

Saying this, it is important to realize that a knee-jerk rejection of the coexistence of rhetoric and philosophy is out of place. On any generous understanding of what philosophy is, the existence of rhetorical strategies in philosophical writing does not rule out philosophy. In fact, the contrary is the case. Philosophy is always rhetorical, but its rhetoric may not always be a focal point of interest. There are some philosophers in whom the rhetorical nature of their enterprise comes to the fore. Schopenhauer is one such philosopher. Kierkegaard and Nietzsche also belong to this company. Kierkegaard is the philosopher of indirection, and Nietzsche of metaphor.

Let us come at these philosophers first by way of a story of their reception in wider philosophical circles. Both philosophers have been outsiders to the dominant forms of philosophical practice for most of their existence. Kierkegaard has remained a marginal figure while Nietzsche has enjoyed bursts of popularity on the continent and is enjoying one in France at the moment. Meanwhile in the "analytic" philosophy departments of mainstream universities in England and America, Nietzsche remains a marginal figure except where "deconstruction" has set in.

It is not clear how Kierkegaard and Nietzsche fit in, or whether they can fit in at all. Perhaps they are not philosophers but romantic poets who write in a philosophical key. They are both so singular that no school can fashion itself after their image. Nor can any existing school incorporate them or coexist with them in easy reciprocity. The barriers to assimilation exist in the writings of Kierkegaard and Nietzsche themselves.

Examples are not hard to find. Kierkegaard is famous for his pseudonyms. We are always discovering, by chance, some manuscript found in a stove by an unknown third party. The words of the manuscript and their author are so removed from normal life that readers can only follow by putting themselves into extreme isolation, and forgetting the consolations of self-deceptive social life.

For Kierkegaard truth is something subjective and experiential, not discursive and general. To convey this truth, therefore, he must eschew discursive and general language. He does not want individuality to be swallowed up by conceptual thought. What is left for him is persuasion. He utilizes the rhetorical and poetic facilities of language indirectly to face each reader with the irreducible singularity of his or her own life. The only communication he is interested in is indirect communication. There can only be a roundabout way of pointing to something which has no public reference.

To anyone who thinks that the expression "private reference" is an oxymoron, and that whatever cannot be said in clear straightforward prose is unintelligible, Kierkegaard is not a philosopher at all, or if he is, then a bad one. To a practice of philosophy which allows only clear straightforward prose, Kierkegaard's tortuous and time-consuming language will likely be met with impatience. That is to be expected.

Impatience is experienced by those who are trying to get

somewhere and are frustrated in doing so. To be prevented from moving quickly is only a problem if one is in a hurry. Perhaps Kierkegaard's greatest feat is to liberate us from the press of present time. To read something like *The Concluding Unscientific Postscript*[8] is like trying to unwind on a deserted beach after a hectic time in the city. At first you have to remember not to run from the water to the bar. Later, if the vacation is long enough, everything slows down. So what if it takes four minutes to reach the bar rather than two? Since there is nowhere to go and nothing to do, you get used to it after a while. So with Kierkegaard's writing, at first it is frustrating because of the desire for quick "edification," but then the slow pace of thought becomes enjoyable in itself. The mind ceases to be in a hurry and therefore has a novel opportunity to look around undistracted by scrambling thoughts.

Whatever the merits of Kierkegaard's philosophical position, there is no doubt as to the centrality of rhetorical and poetic devices in the achievement of the philosophical "effects" produced by his writings. My own view is that Kierkegaard is indeed a philosopher, though one who cannot be schooled, and that the use of indirect communication is legitimate if not inescapable in philosophy.

Kierkegaard is extremely devious in his use of rhetorical strategies and tropes. He makes great use of circumlocution. We are never given formulas or recipes which we can just accept and use. Everything must be questioned, nothing taken for granted. If he speaks about a "leap of faith," it is with no assurance of the outcome. He is not above using invective, satire, irony, jokes, parables, and all the rest to lead us back to ourselves by a circuitous route that only we can follow.

Kierkegaard is concerned with saying the unsayable while aware that it is, in fact, unsayable. In this he differs from the early Wittgenstein who remarked that we should remain silent about that of which we cannot speak. However, we should only remain silent if we are committed to a certain view of language and what it can say. The constraints on the concept of meaning which is built into this view of language limit what can be said and, at the same time, what it makes sense to say. Roughly, the sayable coincides with the expressed content of the positive sciences. Nothing else counts as saying.

Wittgenstein himself became aware of the deficiencies of this view, and interestingly his style becomes noticeably more Kierke-gaardian. His language in the *Investigations*[9] is far more obviously rhetorical. It shocks and surprises a reader with conventional philosophical expectations. The rules of language are open-ended and are always open to adaptation, rejection, or modification. We "play language games" which are embedded in a "form of life." Universals are "family resemblances," and so on. What we have is a series of metaphors which suggest connections between the different themes of the *Investigations*.

Though it would be fair to say that Wittgenstein is always more sparing of rhetorical devices than Kierkegaard, they are still the basis for his later work. To use metaphor signals that language is no longer capable of doing its work in a simple descriptive manner. Metaphors are ambiguous. They can be interpreted in many ways, restricted only by the ingenuity of the interpreter. There is no clear criterion of the truth of an interpretation of a metaphor. There is no literal paraphrase for metaphorical expressions. Metaphors are not just compressed similes. Rather, a metaphor is a central switchboard which links a multitude of incoming and outgoing calls. A live metaphor is one in which the switchboard is hopping with signals. Connections are made all over the place. But once they have been made and everyone is familiar with the relations involved, the metaphor dies and loses its interest.

Neither Wittgenstein nor Kierkegaard is a doctrinaire philoso-pher. Each wants to make the reader responsible for his own thoughts. Each refuses to be taken literally. (This is even true in the *Tractatus*[10] where Wittgenstein bids us throw down the ladder up which we have climbed after we reach the top.) Both philosophers use methods of indirection to bring the readers around to a different way of thinking and seeing things. They are not so much arguing for the truth of some philosophical proposition or other as persuading us to think about things differently.

Nietzsche is a slightly different case. Like Kierkegaard, he stands outside the mainstreams of both continental and Anglo-American philosophy. It is a moot question whether Nietzsche's impact on the French intellectual scene in recent years marks the final incorporation of his thought into a mainstream philosophy, or whether he will prove indigestible even there. He certainly does not fit very comfortably within the traditional stories about philosophy told from within the academic institutions themselves.

Nevertheless, Nietzsche cries out for public recognition as neither Kierkegaard nor Wittgenstein does. He is the outsider saying "Look at me, I'm on the outside and I dare you to come out." He constantly calls attention to his otherness. His going mad at the end, if that is what he did, could not have been scripted better if he had written his life story in advance and then acted it out. The onset of insanity is the boundary line beyond which it is acceptable to dismiss whatever is said.

Nietzsche is an outlaw riding the bad lands of philosophy. From the borders he goes on hit-and-run raids, but he never sticks around for argument. There is nothing fair, balanced, or just about Nietzsche's attacks on religion, philosophy, truth-as-ordinarily-conceived, and traditional moral values. Nietzsche destroys, but as a side-effect we have the exhilaration of feeling ancient prejudices fall away. We have a liberation, but a liberation for what?

Nietzsche is clearer about what this liberation is from than what it is for. The positive things he has to say about how life should be lived must be seen in the vacuum which supports them. Nothing supports the creation of values. This is his claim. But its truth, if it has one, lies outside strict philosophical argumentation.[11] What arguments he does come up with have been severely criticized. Perhaps we should say that Nietzsche is not really a philosopher at all, or maybe just a bad philosopher. Such a judgment is over-hasty. There is more going on in Nietzsche's writing than can be captured in a net of conceptual argumentation. We are certainly unable to understand the impact his writings have had if we look only to the logical validity of his arguments.

Consider his infamous "eternal return of the same."[12] This thought comes to us looking as though it were some kind of bizarre cosmological theory. We could frame it like this. If there is an infinite amount of time, but only a finite set of permutations of matter in time, then there will come a time when matter will be arranged in exactly the same way as it has been arranged at some time in the past. But, of course, every arrangement of matter will recur again and again. Hence we can say, for example, that I have written these very sentences an infinite number of times in the past, and will write them an infinite number of times in the future. If that is true, then it is my fervent wish that my last sentence, and this one too, will bear repetition.

But the point here is not the truth of the matter. Usually, as I understand it, we just need to trot out physically compelling reasons why the thought of such recurrence is nonsensical. That will take care of the problem, and we will not have to come to grips with Nietzsche's claim. Nietzsche himself calls his idea "the most dreadful thought." We are to experience dread when we contemplate the eternal return. Instead of arguing for its truth, Nietzsche asks us to enquire of ourselves whether we can bear the simple thought of the eternal recurrence. The whole thing is nothing but a device for getting us to look at things, including our own lives, in a radically different way.

The rationally minded might take consolation in the fact that if everything is to happen in just the way it has already happened, then the thoughts one thinks will also be the same. Therefore, there will never come a time, even in an infinitely repetitious series, in which the thought of the eternal recurrence will ever be anything more than an abstraction. It can have no other meaning for a thinking person. Certainly one will never be aware of any of the repetitions except in the contemplation of this bizarre hypothesis. Yet it is precisely in the contemplation of this hypothesis that the dread must somehow emerge.

Perhaps through a further sophistication of Nietzsche's idea we can imagine a life parallel to those which exactly repeat themselves. This life is the perpetually growing self-awareness of the same life as lived in infinite repetition. Incapable of actually doing anything, or intervening in the repetitious life, it could only sit there in silent witness of the same scenes over and over again.

At the very time of reading this, or of my writing it, we are both silent witnesses of ourselves. The difference is that you and I have no knowledge of the outcome of our own lives. Our lives will not have an outcome until we are dead, at which time they will no longer be our lives, but someone else's, if anyone's (even if that "someone" is oneself in another guise). The great advantage of our parallel selves is that they are spared this anxiety. Their great disadvantage is that while for us the future is still made up of possibilities, for our parallel selves, they are not. There are no more possibilities.

I shudder to think what I must feel like going through some particularly embarrassing events of my life which I would rather not go into. To think of having to rehearse those times for all perpetuity is indeed dreadful. Of course, it is not so bad to think

31

about reliving the happy times, but how many of those will really stand up to the test of eternity? If one had eternity to re-experience them, progressively knowing more and more about them, growing more familiar with them, would their interest last? That seems a sensible question.

From a certain point of view all this is no more than some philosophical fantasy – philosophy in the mode of science fiction. It is a story about a parallel life which can have for its experience no other content than that provided by the repetitious life upon which it lives parasitically. It is captive to the life of another with which, however, it cannot communicate. For while my parallel self is presumably aware of my thinking all this right now, I cannot be aware of its thinking anything at all, except in a story. Yet the dread that story might inspire still exists, whatever we say about the fiction.

The dread comes of asking whether or not one's life is worth reliving infinitely. Nietzsche states that to say "yes" to one's life eternally relived down to the last detail denotes a state of psychic health. We do not have to go along with him all the way to realize that his "dreadful thought" can have an effect upon how one experiences time. It has an intensifying force which singles out each moment for special scrutiny.

The upshot of this discussion of the eternal recurrence is that Nietzsche's thought has content; it does raise questions and put things in a different perspective, though its intelligibility or truth value is elusive. It is a modern myth, and through it we can still see the power of myth to create effects far in excess of its purely rational content. Plato himself took his hat off to the power of poetry, and acknowledged it as the educator of Greece. He said it issued from a divine mania sent from heaven, but for that very reason it was dark and obscure. Poets do not understand the *logos* of their own speech, another speaks through them. In fact the critics often know more about what the poet says than the poet himself. However, Plato also saw the danger in poetic power because it exists unsubordinated to *logos* or reason. Hence, he turns the poets away from his republic, but with great respect, and he regretfully censors the works of poetic creation. Poetry, he is clear, must be made to hold its genius in check.

Nietzsche's story of the eternal recurrence has that dangerous power which Plato would hold in check. There is something irrational about the effects of Nietzsche's writing which should be guarded against. The production of dread is not part of the rational project of philosophy. That can only be some perlocutionary effect of the illocutionary acts of proper philosophy.

Nietzsche throws down the gauntlet to whoever picks up his writings. He puts the reader on the spot and leaves matters up in the air. The reader is seduced into the heights only to be left hanging without support. His targets are so numerous that all readers are included somewhere. There is an element of satire in Nietzsche's writing which invites the reader to take the high road with him and to scorn the objects of his ridicule. These effects are part of Nietzsche's philosophical rhetoric. His aim is not so much to produce intellectual agreement with a philosophical theory as to shift our whole perspective on the world. For this he needs the techniques of persuasion.

In rhetoric the important issues remain up for grabs even after they are settled by judgment. We cannot extricate them from the perils of contingency. Among these issues are theoretical questions of politics, law, and public relations. Matters of principle are just as real as the legal system which upholds them, but they are subject to misuse, change, and even obliteration. Rhetoric comes into its own where words, formulas, contracts, etc. become a focus of attention, where words create the reality which has objective existence in human institutions, e.g. in courts and assemblies.

It is true that there are many differences between philosophy and institutions such as courts and assemblies. But the points of similarity are striking and suggestive. Let us take the problem of counter-factuals. There is much discussion about how we are to analyze negative conditionals, about the material and formal mode of "if . . . then" statements. To look at the literature is to see a complicated, highly technical, and tightly enclosed world of discourse. It is a world in which the participants are familiar with the same writings, the same references. There are differences of opinion. X writes of Y's reply to Z. Somebody made a mistake here, somebody there. My ignorance of the details of this literature does not affect the more general point that issues are up for grabs in the debates on counter-factuals. There is a toing and froing. Different views catch on, die away, and are reborn in a new debate. (Kripke's reintroduction of the old debate about necessary predicates is a good instance of this.[13]) It would also be fair to say that there are philosophical fashions which sweep all before them, fire up a lot of controversy, and then lose their appeal as something else comes along.

Nietzsche's philosophy is rhetorical because it accepts a rhetorical dimension to philosophical discourse which cannot be erased (or, if it can be, then not without leaving traces). So Nietzsche is not ashamed of using rhetoric to undermine confidence in commonsense thinking and philosophy, and in the superiority of reason as a special access to truth. Common sense and reason have their own rhetoric as well, designed to persuade readers to adopt a certain way of thinking and investigating truth. Nietzsche is doing the same thing, but with all the stops pulled out.

If truth is perspectival as he maintains, then support for truth can only be rhetorical. Even if there is a truth which exists independently of what everyone takes to be true, then "what everyone takes to be true" will still be up for grabs. If what rational philosophy calls "truth" is just a metaphor which has been drained of its life-blood and turned into an abstract concept, then the time is ripe for a full-blooded use of metaphor and rhetoric. Nietzsche can make positive recommendations abut the values it is fitting for a full human being to possess, but only by acknowledging that the "truth" of his recommendations can be settled, and never permanently, in a rhetorical arena alone. Thus he is willing to throw his hat into a ring which those he attacks will not, for the most part, acknowledge.

I have been speaking of philosophical effects as though this were an unproblematical notion. Perhaps it is not so simple. What is the character of philosophical effects which distinguishes them from effects of other kinds? Are not effects the effects of causes? Is it not the case, after all, that the notion of a philosophical effect is nonsensical or self-contradictory? So far as a piece of philosophical writing does produce effects of various kinds in its interpreters, we have something marginal to the philosophical enterprise. That enterprise is a public practice where the object is to bring the speaker's meaning into coincidence with linguistic meaning, where language becomes a window to what is in someone's mind. And that is just the case when words are used in straightforward linguistic communication.

I go up to the bar and order a drink, saying, "Pint of stout, please." I say what I mean, and I mean what I say. We rely, in practice, on this fact. When we want to make sure about it, we bring in lawyers to draw up contracts which all parties sign. By signing a contract you make it known that it is your will that is expressed in the agreement. And even without a contract we rely on others to tell the truth and make their intentions known and understood.

It seems reasonable to acknowledge, therefore, that straightforward linguistic communication is a practical necessity of life. We must live on the assumption that at least in conventional settings, people will behave in certain predictable ways. This includes the kinds of speech acts which are likely to make sense in different conventional settings. How we take the remarks addressed to us by others depends crucially on what we take the situation to be. One of the determinates of the situation is what the speaker says, the words he or she utters, and the presumption that the words are meant in earnest.

This is fine as far as straightforward linguistic communication can take us. However, it is not far enough. I will argue that though straightforward linguistic communication is a practical necessity of our social life, there is more to life than sheer practicality. If we look closely at the contexts in which straightforward linguistic communication is most appropriate, we will see that they are, broadly speaking, instrumental contexts. Means and ends are adjusted through speech. It is an area of pragmatic concerns, in which it is what needs doing that is the center of interest.

There are two points to be made straight off. Not all communication is instrumental. Not all instrumental communication is straightforward. To use my favorite example, if I go into a bar to order a drink, and I do not know the bar or the bar person, my communication will succeed on a purely functional level. I might be more sociable and have a chat, but if I want a drink, I must make at least two things clear to the person behind the bar; one is that I want a drink, the other is what drink I want. These are the bare bones of a primarily functional, instrumental, conventional speech act which I have called straightforward linguistic communication.

As Wittgenstein and Austin so forcefully point out, people do things with words. Speaking is acting, and often speaking makes something so. Wittgenstein contrasts the image of language on

35

holiday with that of language in its ordinary use.[14] Its ordinary use marks out the boundaries of straightforward linguistic communication. In such situations language is most at home and least problematic. It becomes problematic, according to Wittgenstein, when language goes on holiday, when words are asked to pull unnatural loads. The standard language of philosophy is puzzling if considered from the point of view of the ordinary use of words in straightforward linguistic communication. There, at any rate, words are doing a real job of work.

In *How to Do Things with Words*[15] J.L. Austin speaks of illocutionary action to mark out the field of linguistic communication. He delineates the world of working words. An illocutionary act is one which is performed in saying something, one in which the words uttered have a bearing upon the success of the act. For example, saying "I promise" in the appropriate circumstances is just to make a promise. Saying "Dig a hole there" just is an order if it is issued by someone with the authority to give one.

Austin made a number of useful distinctions which will help us in our inquiry. It is worth spending a moment on them. Illocutionary acts are distinguished on the one hand from locutionary, and on the other from perlocutionary acts. The locutionary act consists of uttering a syntactically and semantically well-formed string of words (having "sense" and "reference"). The perlocutionary act consists in the production of effects in the hearer which are not directly related to the success of the speech-act in question. One difference between illocutionary and perlocutionary actions is that the former can be made explicit with no loss of success, whereas the latter are not as transparent.

One of Austin's main points is that we have resources within language to make our illocutionary acts explicit. If there is any doubt, we have the means to make the force of our utterance known by the use of an explicit illocutionary force indicator. For example, if I am in some doubt as to whether you took my reference to the bull in the field you are standing in as a warning, I can make it clear by saying "I warn you that there is a bull in the field." Or you can ask me, "Was that a warning or a statement?" Sometimes, as in legal contracts, explicit illocutionary verbs are used in order to avoid misunderstandings. Verbal formulas help to define the context in which they operate effectively. Think of the rules of debate in consultative bodies or in courts of law.

However, it is not hard to find examples of instrumental communication which are far from straightforward. A paradigm, perhaps, would be the speech of the con artist. The con artist is interested, precisely, in making sure that what is said and what is meant never fully coincide. And yet his conversation has purposes which are fulfilled in the use and manipulation of others through a false identity constituted primarily through speech. On a more mundane level we have speech with ulterior motives: we have badgering, pestering, blackmailing, insinuating, persuading, and so on.

Instrumental interactions are finitely teleological. There is a particular end which is the target of action, the object of some intention. For the con artist this will involve others doing or thinking certain things. I have an intention only another can fulfill. I must get the other to do what I want or think what I want, but that other must not realize that I am trying to get him or her to do or think those things. Hence the use of indirect means, of persuasive arguments, hints, suggestions, and all the other devices which can be used to entrap the unwary.

The con artist has a scheme for making himself rich, let us say, by setting up a dummy company and then milking the unsuspecting of their money. To do this he must push the means of persuasion to their limits, for he has nothing but patter with which to convince the unwary of his veracity. The con artist has few props. His objects must be accomplished through language, and he could be said to have a purely verbal vocation. The usual story has it that the con artist uses the greed and gullibility of his victims to trap them in his scheme. So an efficient one must be good at spotting the greedy and the gullible and then at exploiting their personalities for his own gain.

The con artist uses language in such a way as to speak what is false and have it taken as true, and to manipulate the victim's self-image and sense of self-esteem. The con artist might say, for example, "I wouldn't tell everyone this, but the smart money's moving into company X. Don't tell anyone, now." Rhetorically, these two sentences simultaneously stimulate greed, imply the possession of intelligence in the hearer, make the hearer a part of something secret, and make the hearer feel like a dummy if he were to pass up the opportunity to buy. This is false eloquence, but eloquence none the less. The factually false proposition, that the smart money's moving into company X, is part of the deception, but equally important are the other appeals and presuppositions on which the con artist depends.

The conclusion is that instrumental communication can be very devious indeed; in that case it specializes in the use of indirect means of persuasion. The con artist's use of language to exploit others, the blatantly rhetorical structures he employs, and the outright deceit involved have earned him a hard place in history. Plato's criticisms of the sophists and rhetoricians tar them with the same brush as the con artist. Both are reprehensible because they use language to deceive and exploit the gullible. Both use words as instruments in the completion of their projects, which lie outside what they say.

Plato's claim is that speaking is good, not for its own sake, but for some good extrinsic to itself. He does allow that good speeches are to be constructed to praise the gods and the heroes and warriors of the *polis*. But the end here, as always for Plato, is the common good. Good speeches, that is artful speeches, are good when put to antecedently good ends, namely ends which are good for the state and its citizens. What is wrong with rhetoric is that its very forms are so well suited to misuse. Plato is offended by the ease with which rhetorical devices can be put to the service of personal ends and the detrimental effects those practices have on the *polis*.

However, not all communication is instrumental, whether straightforward or indirect. People speak together for a variety of different reasons and they are not always trying to get someone to do or think something for reasons of their own. Speaking is a kind of doing, but it can also be a way of being together with others. It can be a way of passing the time. Telling stories, relating gossip, sympathizing with another's plight, and so on, can all be ways of being together.

Non-instrumental communication takes place for the most part during pauses in the day. Speaking which is constitutive of being with another requires a space maintained outside the press of practical concerns. This does not mean, however, that our "time-out" with others is of negligible importance. The setting up of "social occasions" is one of the major preoccupations of human beings. Whether it is sharing a work-break, sitting down to tea, or going to a party, it is clear that there are numerous occasions for the commencement and maintenance of non-instrumental communication.

Let us go back to the bar, but this time suppose it to be the local. Mr K, then, goes into his local bar at his usual time on an ordinary day. He is going to get a drink no doubt, but unless he is an alcoholic, that will not be this only reason for going to the bar. He is going because it is Tuesday afternoon and he always goes to his local on Tuesdays. His friends are there. He knows the bartender. It would not be his local if he did not like the people there and fit in with them. For Mr K and the other locals, it is like a home away from home. Let us imagine this anyway.

Now it may very well be that Mr K figures that old Jones might be putting in an appearance this afternoon. A likely time, perhaps, to remind Jones that he still has not returned the garden shears. This is a practical matter and the pretext for an instrumental act of communication with old Jones. But that is not the reason for going to the pub either. It is a combination of many things. And if we further imagine a rustic pub rather than an executive club in town where deals are constantly made, we have the setting for non-instrumental, non-exploitative interaction and communication.

Another way into this non-instrumental area of communication is through a further investigation of speech acts, and in particular speech acts which set out to describe the world. As we will see, the descriptive practices which are supported by language can function in both instrumental and non-instrumental contexts of action. In one context language is used to perform actions which are instrumental in the carrying out of some project. In the other, language is used to carry out the project of "being together" in a certain mode. The mode most relevant to our immediate interests will be that of story telling, and the descriptive practices displayed therein.

Some of our speech acts can rightly be called illocutionary acts of describing the world. There are, to borrow Wittgenstein's metaphor, language-games of describing.[16] Those games will determine what counts as a good description and what a bad one, internal to the game which is played. Thus if I were asked to describe an internal combustion engine, the correct description would be one which sets out the salient features. I would not have to describe the parts of any particular engine, but I would have to describe a part which has the function of a carburettor. No internal combustion engine can get along without one.

Consider now a different case, say that of describing a unicorn. Unicorns have often been described, and yet they do not exist. So does that mean that it is not possible to list the things which need to be mentioned to make the description a good one? A bad description of an internal combustion engine would leave out any reference to the carburettor. A bad description of a unicorn would leave out all mention of its distinctive horn. We all know that unicorns look very much like horses with single horns projecting from their foreheads. We are told they have magic powers. We know that they figure in fairy tales and the like.

Obviously the standards of correctness which apply in the case of descriptions of engines do not apply in the case of unicorns. Yet there are standards for the correctness of unicorn descriptions internal to the tales in which they appear.

There is a sense in which the speech act of describing is a conventional act. Austin identifies this with the resources in language which allow us to make explicit the "force" of our utterances, what we are doing in saying something.[17] The fact that the meaning of words in a language is stable, though changing, indicates an independence of word meaning from any particular speaker's actions or intentions. For example, if my audience takes me to be giving a description of something, I will be held responsible for using my words with their general acceptation. In fact, if it were not for this general acceptance of the meaning of our words, we would never be able to discuss the nature of language or anything else.

However, the independence of word meaning is not unqualified. It is only a relative independence which marks the place of convention in linguistic practice. Words, as Austin says, have no meaning outside a sentence. The meanings we find in dictionaries tell us how a word is used correctly in different contexts. This correct use is simply the conventionally recognized one. But conventions change over time, and so does the meaning of words. Obsolete words come back into use, their meanings separated from their original contexts and attached to new ones. Or, in another fashion, the objects which were spoken of in an age gone by disappear, and the words whose use was tied to the existence of those objects will no longer signify anything to us.

Imagine an earth so radically changed by pollution that the surface became uninhabitable. Suppose underground shelters become the permanent home for a remnant of the human species. There are books and films, but many of the objects which used to be found on the surface of the earth are no longer there. As the generations of those who can personally remember the surface die off, what connection can the succeeding generations have to that non-existent place? The films of the long dead earth cease to have any connection with the world, and old earth becomes a place of myth. There is no longer any occasion to use those words outside of a ritual context radically divorced from that in which those words first found civil employment.

But more than this, the language-games of description are just one of many sets of language-games centered on different though often related practices. There are also ordering and warning, promising and exhorting, apologizing and congratulating, and a host of others. Each of these families is broken down again into the many family members, each with its own idiosyncrasies. These are the straightforward actions which it is possible to perform in speaking to others in the appropriate circumstances.

Most, but not all, of these language-games have their home in pragmatic, instrumental communication contexts. But some, like the language-game of describing fictional creatures, take place outside the practical arena of straightforward linguistic communication. However, there is no particular problem about words at play in fairy-tales. Words, there, are employed about a non-existent world. We understand this when we understand it as a fairy-tale.

However, it is precisely because the description of unicorns takes place in a playful linguistic environment that talk about such things is, or can be, a form of communication which lies outside of an instrumental pragmatic context. Talk about unicorns and other poetic creations takes place in a space carved out of the day where the press of time and events is temporarily suspended.

Words at play set up the possibility for occasions of non-instrumental communication which can afford the linguistic time and space for indirection. When it is time to sit down and listen to a story, a space is created which is ready to receive it. Brackets are placed around a moment set aside for enjoyment and wonder. We can imagine that in traditional oral cultures people sat down to listen to the bard after the work of the day was over and everyone had been fed. Then came the time to listen to tales of heroes, gods, and lovers.

41

Philosophical discussions take place in a space carved out of the day, in much the same way as a fairy-tale or story. Perhaps Wittgenstein is right to say that in philosophy words go on holiday. But he may be wrong to conclude that this is to the disadvantage of philosophy. Consider whether we should see this not as some kind of defect in philosophy (now seen as a kind of fiction), but as the condition for the possibility of indirection in philosophical writing. For it is when language goes on holiday, when it leaves its pragmatic concerns, that there is time to play around with devices of rhetoric and poetry and explore the philosophical effects which can be produced by the use of words.

The rhetorical dimension of philosophy centers on the notion not of an illocutionary act, but of perlocutionary action, what someone does by saying something, not in saying it. There is no difference in this respect between the philosopher and the con artist. They both employ indirect means of communication, one from the motivation of gaining advantage, the other more in a spirit of play and exploration. To connect philosophy with play is not a frivolous gesture. Play can be serious, but it keeps its relation with fantasy and imagination and allows for the ingenious making of novel and broad connections between unlikely terms. Through play and a kind of imaginative reconstruction of thought, the practice of philosophical discussion can alter one's understanding of the world and one's attitude toward it.

Let us explore the notion of perlocutionary action and its role in philosophical rhetoric. The distinction arose in connection with Austin's discussion of illocutionary acts. After his analysis of conventional speech acts, Austin realized that something more is done with words than can be made explicit with an illocutionary verb.[18] Perlocutionary actions are those which aim at effects in the audience which cannot be accomplished through the possession of linguistic competence alone.

Austin tries various ways to make the distinction and various tests to find out which actions are illocutionary and which are perlocutionary. But since his main interest is in illocutionary actions, his account of perlocutionary speech is sketchy at best. There is a rough and ready linguistic criterion to demarcate the two types of speech acts that will suffice for the rough and ready sense needed here.

I have already used the formulation without mentioning it. An illocutionary act is one that can be accomplished in saying something. A perlocutionary act is one which is accomplished, not in saying something, but by saying something. Of course illocutionary actions are not successful simply in the saying of something. There are other conditions as well. The speaker must secure uptake, that is capture the attention of the hearer. And he must make plain the force of what he says, whether it is a warning, a promise, or what have you. Finally, he must make plain the content of the act: in the case of a warning, what the danger is of which the hearer should be aware, or in the case of a promise, what is being promised.

With the case of perlocutionary acts, all these conditions together cannot in themselves bring about the desired effect. For example, if someone speaks loudly to one presumed partly deaf, who unbeknownst to the speaker has recently acquired a hearing aid, now turned up to the maximum volume, saying "The tea is ready," this might have the effect of startling the hearer. This case is instructive on a number of points.

First, it is not the case that the speaker startles the hearer in saying "The tea is ready." "To startle" is not an illocutionary verb. "I startle you that x" is not a felicitous expression. Furthermore, the way this story is told, the speaker intended to inform the hearer that it was time to have a cup of tea, not to startle him. Nevertheless, his spoken words had this effect, which transcended his intentions. The speaker did not mean to startle the hearer but did so, none the less. The effect, so to speak, escapes the control of the speaker.

Speech acts share this feature with action in general, that when we set out to do something intentionally, unintended effects are produced. We can never rely on the certainty of our plans maturing in exactly the way we anticipate. Speech and action in general take place in a contingent environment. Plans go wrong and unexpected obstacles arise. We continue to act in further uncertain circumstances, adapting what we do to the changing situation. And this situation is as much created by our own actions, including our speech actions, as it is by the unforeseen events which come our way and can never be totally prevented or controlled. (These will include the actions, including speech actions, of others.)

In some ways our example of the speaker who inadvertently

startles the hearer does not illuminate a large enough area for our purposes, for the speaker in the example did not mean to startle the hearer, but to do something very different. Yet it is possible to form the intention of startling someone. How is this possible? Saying "I'm trying to startle you" does not look like a good tactic for actually startling someone. To admit to having that project will alert the hearer to what the speaker is trying to do. Of course, nothing prevents a hearer from becoming startled anyway, but it will not come about through the project of the speaker. The situation will be the same as in our previous example, where the speaker inadvertently produced an effect in the hearer outside of his intention. The difference is that here the intention of the speaker is manipulative. The speaker tries to startle the hearer and says things the speaker thinks will bring this effect about. But if the hearer is startled by something which is no device of the speaker's, then the speaker's intention to startle is not fulfilled even though the hearer is, in fact, startled.

What if someone said "I startle you because your shoes are on fire"? That might work, but it would be because of the burning shoes, not anything the speaker said. However, if you looked down and saw no fire, you would likely think the whole thing a joke. Nevertheless, it is possible to succeed in the attempt to startle someone, not directly, but obliquely. Someone who is trying to have some effect on another wants to have some role in the production of that effect. X can only achieve the object of startling Y indirectly, but would like to have some part in producing that effect.

Suppose I know as a matter of empirical fact that loud noises startle people. I might try to startle someone by making a loud noise under appropriate circumstances. But how do I know what the appropriate circumstances are? Perhaps I notice that people tend to be startled by a loud noise when they least expect it. So now I take two cymbals, sneak up on someone quietly contemplating a tree, and bang them together six inches behind that person's head. Chances are very good that I will succeed in startling the person. I could also yell "Fire!" in a crowded cinema and have a good chance of startling at least some of the patrons. In both cases indirect means are used to produce an effect in a hearer. The former is rather crude, but the latter is worth further investigation.

To yell "Fire!" in a crowded cinema is an almost conventional means of inducing panic. It can be a warning, perhaps a description, but there is nothing in the illocutionary force of "Fire!", even in a crowded cinema, which by itself generates panic. The proper response to a warning is to become more perceptive, alert, and on guard, not to panic blindly.

The intentions with which "Fire!" is yelled in a crowded cinema can differ, and yet the effect be the same. Someone might yell "Fire!" in order to warn the people of the danger. They panic. Someone yells "Fire!" and wants to start a panic. The people panic. The former attempted a straightforward speech act and failed. The latter tried an indirect speech act and succeeded. There must be something about the thought of danger in a crowded cinema that communicates fear and panic and which can be used to induce those states.

One of the good things about straightforward linguistic communication is that meaning appears there in a more or less transparent fashion. Yelling "Fire!" in a crowded cinema to induce a panic is a dirty trick. In general we do not like people using language to prey on our sentiments. We do not like to be the object of a causal process which bypasses our awareness. We are in the area that Anscombe called "mental causation."[19] I find myself walking up and down and realize that marching music caused me to start marching without my noticing it.

Consider another example. Suppose we know someone who cannot sit still when a certain kind of music is played. When that music is played this person's feet keep time to it. Suppose further that we know someone who refuses to believe this and is willing to wager on it. We might then as an experiment so arrange things as to have that sort of music played when we are relaxing with the person about whom we have the bet. We know that the music is coming on, and when it does we determine whether the subject's feet are tapping out the beat. If they are, we win the bet. If not, we lose. But in either case the whole transaction takes place far from any awareness of the subject. If we won the bet, we could "make" the subject tap out rhythms unknowingly any time we wanted to. This is a clear case of manipulation. And it would not work if the plan were revealed. For if warned beforehand that this music was coming up and that there was a bet on that he could not keep still, he would probably be able to refrain from tapping his foot through a conscious effort.

Indirect instrumental communication consists in the use of perlocutionary devices to bring about effects in hearers without coming clean about what is being done. This is what is objected to in such communication. There is something underhanded about the whole business. Nevertheless, it is possible to carry perlocutionary projects to completion with a high degree of sophistication. There is only a difference of degree between the most sophisticated case and yelling "Fire!" in a crowded cinema. In both we find empirical regularities which can be empirically investigated and the results stated. This is one of the reasons why Plato castigates rhetoric and sophistry. They are not true arts, he says, but mere knacks gained from experience (*empeiros*). The rhetorician here is thought of as a master of indirect instrumental communication. He knows all the tricks which can be gleaned from experience to bring about effects in hearers which can be shaped, maneuvered, and directed by the use of rhetorical devices.

Perhaps another objection Plato would raise is that of the pragmatism inherent in rhetorical projects. I have mentioned that rhetoric traditionally covers those human affairs which are open to manipulation through human choice and action. This is the contingent world of unforeseen consequences I mentioned earlier. The rhetorician is restricted to what works in changing empirical circumstances. He never attains knowledge, nor would real knowledge, in truth, be of any use to him. But he is a master of indirection. He is so good at it that he has given indirect communication a bad name. This must have been one of Plato's worries.

However, these worries should not be restricted to indirect instrumental communication alone. Plato's dialogues are themselves rhetorical. Therefore, if philosophy is seen to have an indissoluble link with rhetoric, the negative valuations attaching to the former will also attach to the latter. However, if we understand that philosophy takes place in a non-instrumental space, the negative points about an instrumental rhetoric will no longer have the same application. In that space language use is freed from the press of specific first-order concerns. Rhetoric, there, is the use of such devices as metaphor, metonymy, synecdoche, and irony to produce the *philosophical effects* of philosophical writing.

These philosophical effects are distinguished from rhetorical effects pure and simple by the absence of an instrumental context of their use. Furthermore, these devices are the very same ones employed by proper rhetoricians in the negative sense. This is very confusing, since we can find nothing in the indirect means of communication themselves to prevent us practicing a rhetoric of specific and immediate ends. Philosophical effects of philosophy writing or speaking are those produced not through deception, nor yet transparently, but through philosophical tropes or figures by which means the mind is persuaded to think another way or explore an unanticipated avenue of investigation.

These philosophical tropes are very like the old notion of "figures of thought" in the manuals of rhetoric. Rhetorical strategies are laid out to prepare the reader to accept or at least to entertain a certain thought, theory, or hypothesis. They may not be "fore-grounded" in the text, but they are there. This much indirection is necessary for any philosophical position to become articulate. It must address itself to an audience and work within the ambit of ideas shared by both the writer and the projected audience.

Indirect communication becomes more necessary the further the audience is meant to go beyond the familiar confines of its own mental landscape. Perlocutionary action is needed to clear a space for the delivery of difficult, odd, or new-fangled ideas. Philosophical investigation relies upon the lush tropical resources of language to provide the devices needed to produce its effects.

Let us take as a case study the work of Descartes, usually thought of as the born enemy of humanist rhetoric. In many ways this is true, so that if a philosophical rhetoric remains in Descartes' writings, that will be evidence to support the view that rhetoric is ineradically present in philosophical writing.

It is true that Descartes separates his philosophy from rhetoric at numerous points. Perhaps the most famous is a passage from the *Discours de la méthode* (1637) which is worth quoting in full.

> I rated oratory highly and I loved poetry, but I also thought that the one as the other are more talents of the mind than fruits of studies. Those who possess the greatest powers of judgement and the greatest ability to arrange their thoughts in order to make them clear and comprehensible will, at any time, also be the best to persuade other people of what they propose even if they were speaking only in a low Brittany dialect and had never studied oratory.[20]

According to a commonly accepted story Descartes proposed a method by which knowledge can be acquired without depending upon unpredictable "talents of the mind." What is Descartes' conception of those talents of the mind which he attributes to poets and rhetoricians? Primarily, I suspect, these are the talents of invention and arrangement, the ability to use the classical topics to devise a structured speech on any given subject.

To understand Descartes' antipathy to rhetoric we must understand something of its history and its place in his world. One point of difference between theoretical philosophy and rhetoric is that rhetoric, as Aristotle said, belongs to the realm of probable argument. In this, rhetoric is a species of practical reasoning which stops short of certainty. It is a profoundly "timely" intervention into the affairs of the world. Descartes, on the contrary, thought that though the productions of poets and rhetoricians might bring us pleasure, their role in uncovering truth is minimal. For Descartes what matters is scientific or metaphysical knowledge, and both of these investigations are supposed to lead us to certain ahistorical truths about the physical world, the human mind, and God.

To attain these ends Descartes had to reject rhetorical strategies in favor of a method which guarantees results because it transcends the "timely" arena of rhetorical interventions. We do not have to dress the truth up to make it palatable to the imagination and to the desire for pleasure. What we need is a logical means of progression which builds upon what is certain and then extends our reasoning through the minute steps of argument. The method grinds slowly so that nothing will be left out, and there are continuous reviews to see that each step has been properly taken. Anyone with the barest rational facility should be able to make progress in philosophy and science.

It is analogous to learning language. A baby need not be a genius to learn language. This is one of the striking features of language acquisition. Anyone with a properly functioning brain and motor system can learn any language with ease. Even Basque children, who reportedly have to learn one of the most complex languages on earth, manage to learn it in the normal time, about three or four years. Learning language is a basic human capacity and IQ has very little to do with it.

Another point in the analogy is that language is learnt without the benefit of the ornate form of rhetoric found in the seventeenth century. If we took that as the sort of speech spoken to children, it is not clear that they would ever learn their language. The oratorical language of the time is so lush with tropes, circumlocutionary formulas, and copious deliveries, that even the simplest statements would be lost on children with no prior knowledge of the language deformed by oratory.

In the case of learning language it would seem that there must be straightforward linguistic communication before the deformations of poetry and rhetoric can make sense. One must already speak the day-to-day language spoken around one before it is possible to appreciate poetry or rhetoric and respond to its power. It was, we recall, the sophists, not the speakers themselves or the general audience, who sat down to note how effective speakers achieved their successes. It was they who wrote handbooks for effective speaking and who codified the various arguments and styles used in rhetorical practice.

The difference between the first sophists and the audiences they observed is like that between a relatively naïve cinema audience and the professional critic in their midst. The audience responds immediately to the images, music, acting, and words of a film. They are actively engaged in it. The critic is one step removed from all this, and must find it difficult not to become jaded. The critic knows all the tricks in the book, has seen it all before. Where the audience will be biting their nails unreservedly during the obligatory chase sequence, the critic will be biting the nails of one hand only, while writing with the other. If the sequence is a taut one, the critic will call attention to its success; if not, its failure to create suspense. Either way, the critic remains detached from the film.

The sophist and the critic are observers. They watch the productions of speakers or of the film industry and the reactions of audiences, and try to become reflective about what is going on. This, no doubt, is a legitimate thing to do; but the arena of oratory and film is the probable, and thus to become reflective in the required way will do nothing to advance us toward the truth which lies outside the probable, "timely" world of oratory and film.

Again, as with Plato, what Descartes has against rhetoric and oratory is their connection with the uncertain practicalities of life facing each of us. Truths which we can know must lie beyond them and deal with what is certain. Truth speaks for itself and requires no ornate costume. The best speakers will be those who can communicate the truth in a clear and comprehensible manner.

Nevertheless, though Descartes argues that truth speaks for itself regardless of dialect, his topic is persuasion, and persuasion is in the domain of rhetoric. What is the passage which I quoted, if not itself a brilliant piece of rhetoric? It is part of a rhetorical strategy on Descartes' part to discredit an opportunistic and pragmatic rhetoric which he deplores. He uses rhetoric against rhetoric itself. The passage is very well written, powerful, convincing. It deals explicitly with how "the greatest powers of judgement" can seek to be persuasive, which is an ancient rhetorical concern. The truth must persuade us, but someone must first speak the truth. So the truth must be composed for public scrutiny and will never appear without clothes. Those clothes are the arrangements of thoughts in the medium of speech or writing. But his notion of the arrangement of material is precisely one of the two main areas of rhetorical activity. First we must discover arguments and then we must arrange them in an effective order.

Descartes does not let us fall asleep. On the contrary, he enlivens his prose with humor by bringing in what I suppose he takes to be the least oratorical speech imaginable, low Brittany. That image and its contrast with high oratory provide us with a wealth of associated thoughts and images with which we can think about and reconstruct in imagination, Descartes' anti-poetic, anti-rhetorical position.

The dialect of low Brittany is spoken by a person from a region of France far from the Parisian hub of things. People there, I imagine, go in for plain speaking with very little artifice and no conscious artifice at all. Such people are down-to-earth, unsophisticated, not of the city, not very well educated in the liberal arts. Images provided by the idea of "those who had studied oratory" are the reverse. Here we have an urbanized, well-educated sophisticate who moves in very different circles.

Descartes' desire to found a method of gaining knowledge is a sober one. From his perspective the speech of orators and poets seems to be a distraction from the serious business of uncovering truth. The orator wears the right dress and says the right words, but in an arena beneath the dignity of philosophy. The orator is too much of a fop. Descartes is reacting to the excesses of a rhetoric which distinguished itself on the side of style alone and was seen to be indifferent to the content of its thought.

If we look closely at the quoted passage, Descartes takes from the rhetorical tradition what he finds of value there without, however, acknowledging his debt. For example, clarity and comprehensibility (in the sense of making oneself understood) are both goals of traditional rhetoric, as is the emphasis upon the arrangement of thought, which Descartes himself underlines. In other words, he goes to the grab bag of rhetoric, takes what suits his purposes, and then condemns the rest of rhetoric for dealing with mere style and wit, not philosophical truth.

What Descartes leaves out is the inventive and affective side of rhetoric. Truth must persuade us without the use of tricks. We are not children who must have fairy-tales and stories. We do not need images, only the clarity of conceptual thought. The sole part of rhetoric of any use is that dealing with argumentation. Ingenuity is of small importance. We are not to follow word-play but stick to clear and distinct perceptions.

By this means part of rhetoric is hived off as an expansion of logic, leaving, for a now impoverished rhetoric, nothing but ornament and display. Rhetoric is left with "delivery," but with nothing left to deliver.

Descartes says that he began by admiring oratory and loving poetry but ended up doubting their cognitive worth. He does not think that to pursue them is a reliable way of gaining knowledge. At one time, however, he took pleasure in reading or listening to poetry and was stirred by the speeches of the orators. He must have felt their pull and wondered at the skill which produced them.

The trouble with poetry and oratory is that they stand too close to fantasy. Descartes wants a knowledge which is immune to doubt. Neither the wit nor the pathos of tropical language can serve a useful function here. The opposite is true. Wit and the play of pathos obscure the truth for they are not based on observation but upon the unequal "talents of the mind." Descartes, as we saw, is interested in those who possess "the greatest powers of judgement" and whose discernment is based upon solid study and not talent alone.

A pedagogy is implicitly contained in Descartes' epistemology and metaphysics. The truths we can know are universal and at least hypothetically necessary. They are therefore capable of being

51

taught to everyone by the same method. These are truths which can be known on the basis of clear and distinct ideas. Clear and distinct ideas are the same for anyone who attends to them, and can therefore serve as the basis for rational argument. We do not have to search the handbooks and compendia for what the ancients said. There is no need to look up authorities, for the reason in us makes us all authorities. Hence we must judge for ourselves. When it comes to clear and distinct ideas everyone will agree; for the reason in us, though not equally developed, is equally reason in everyone. The light of reason is universal, though not universally developed.

Therefore the truths which are based on clear and distinct ideas will be universal and acceptable to all. No special "talent of the mind" beyond the bare ability to think analytically is required to grasp them. They will not need to be dressed up in any special way to be persuasive. Hence, it will not matter that they are spoken in low Brittany or any other plain dialect.

Descartes has a method to teach and it does not matter what language it is in as long as it is clear and comprehensible. We analyze things to find out how they work. We endlessly churn out analyses on any subject that can withstand discussion. So along with Descartes' method comes a pedagogy which will strip the old syllabuses of their ancient *bricolage*. We do not need all the baggage. We do not have to remember what Pausanias said when Alcibiades stole half his silver plate. Cicero and Quintilian can pass into obscurity. It does not matter any more, not since Descartes invented his method.

When Descartes rummages around in rhetoric and takes out what he wants, he leaves "ingenuity" or "invention" behind. We do not have to be ingenious but perceptive. We must see what is there rather than make up what we want. This idea of rhetorical invention is an important one for our study. My thesis is that despite being maligned and ignored, invention has never been absent from even the most boring of philosophical writings. Rhetorical and philosophical invention have been maligned or ignored, but never without reason.

In its most extravagant forms invention has been rightly criticized. Descartes was looking at late and tired forms of rhetoric. He confused the rhetorical practice then current with what rhetoric is, namely the means of providing something for thought to get hold of, something concrete, an image, a scrap of language, or a feeling. Human inventiveness has supplied us with all the raw materials of further reflection. Later I will argue that the most powerful supplier of these materials is the invention of metaphors which can stretch our imagination and understanding of the world. For the moment, however, all we need is a sense of rhetoric which transcends the purely ornamental version which fancies itself the pinnacle and perfection of a humane education.

Despite everything, Descartes writes with a great rhetorical flair. He also shows himself to be extremely inventive. He displays those "talents of the mind" which he found so superfluous in poetry and rhetoric. There is his famous vision of a new science and philosophy. There is his dream. The *Meditations* is full of memorable images and metaphors. It is written on the model of a religious retreat.[21] There is narration, a story. The philosophy of Descartes, which is to transcend the need for rhetoric, comes to us in the form of a fable. The straight "philosophy" of the *Meditations* is not some hard nut which can be extracted from the husk. On the contrary, the philosophy of Descartes plays its role in the story of the *Meditations* along with all its other elements. The philosophy can only be grasped within a wider dramatic context which Descartes provides to intensify his philosophical objectives.

Descartes sees himself as starting something new in philosophy. His goal is to detach philosophy from the skirts of theology and set it up in its own right. The theory of clear and distinct ideas, the method of acquiring knowledge, the step-by-step procedures, all come together to provide a new basis for carrying out investigations into the nature of things. This new method, it is true, cuts at the roots of the old rhetorical tradition in that it eschews authority, wise sayings, and ornate figures of speech in order to place each individual inquirer on his or her own. We are to rely upon our reason and perception and take nothing on trust.

The problem here, as with any attempt to start something new, is to prepare an audience to receive it. Despite his disclaimers, Descartes is in the rhetorical position of having to create his audience out of whole cloth. He must bring it about that his readers abandon their preconceived ideas, break with their prejudices, and begin to think along new lines. Both the *Meditations* and the *Discourse on Method* serve this rhetorical function; and this function is not simply, or merely, rhetorical but philosophical as well.

Descartes carries out this rhetorical strategy by presenting the reader with startling language and a series of vivid images to help break with previous molds of thought. Two instances are worth recalling here. One is a vivid image and the other a rhetorical question. The image is that of the deceiving demon. The question is whether life might not be a dream and we the dreamers.[22]

Consider the image of the deceiving demon. (By an image I do not mean merely a mental picture, but anything which will serve as a focus of meaning and reflection. Stories may contain images within them.) Normally in a philosophy seminar the hypothesis of the deceiving demon is set in the context of the question of skepticism. Descartes himself sets it up this way. We are to imagine the existence of an extremely powerful being who is capable of representing to us that which does not exist. Now among my representations are those which purport to pick out objects in the "external world," objects which include my very body. The deceiving demon, who controls my representations, makes it appear that these things have a real existence outside my representations of them. What I take to be true is false for I have been misled.

Descartes goes further than this at one point in the *Meditations*.[23] He argues that the deceiving demon might even be able to deceive me about simple arithmetical operations. The equals sign becomes opaque; somehow it marks a forgetting of what is on the other side. I forget that it is "$2 + 2$" which is on the other side of the equal sign in the formula "$2 + 2 = 4$." The "4" which I think to be the sum of that which lies on the other side of the equals sign is not that but something else. The representations of memory are also controlled by the deceiving demon. Hence our memories are not a sure guide to what went before, even in a mathematical operation.

The image of the deceiving demon is a striking one, but its force in a discussion of Descartes' philosophy is not a "strictly philosophical" one. The deceiving demon is discussed because it has pedagogic uses. Teachers and students can use the deceiving demon hypothesis to elicit and connect many of the issues of the *Meditations*. We can use its image to focus on the question of skepticism and knowledge, just as Descartes uses it to sharpen his own solution to the problem of skepticism. Discussion of the deceiving demon is a way to prepare students to understand Descartes' philosophy. It is a rhetorical device with a philosophical point.

Consider again the role of the deceiving demon in the *Meditations*. The supposition that a deceiving demon exists caps a series of escalating doubts about the veracity of what we ordinarily call human knowledge. We start gently enough, it seems, when we are asked to discard all our superstitious beliefs. After this we are to suppose that all the words of wisdom ever spoken might, after all, be false. People do speak falsely, even when they think they are speaking the truth. They may even lie falsely, mistaken in their belief of what is true. So we must not rely on what people say to give us access to the truth. After this slow build-up our doubt is to become more radical. Our senses deceive us from time to time. Perhaps they deceive us all the time. Just this is enough to cast our sense perceptions into doubt. Then the deceiving demon comes to wrap all doubts together and give them the utmost force. Little by little we are led to give up more and more of our world until there is nothing left. And it is at that point that Descartes' "solution" to the problem of the deceiving demon has the most force. Let skepticism run its course; then, if anything remains firm in this flux, we can hold on to it with the utmost confidence.

The deceiving demon prepares the way for the *cogito*. This preparation, however, is not simply philosophical but rhetorical. This can be seen clearly in its very weakness as a hypothesis. If taken straight in its strongest form, it is not convincing. You will recall that the deceiving demon is to make us mistake even our mathematical reasonings. How plausible is this? It is easy to see that if you are trying to add up a long column of numbers, there is always a chance that somewhere down the line you might make a mistake which will carry along and show up in the result. Descartes warns us of this very fact in outlining his method. We are to review and recheck each stage of the operation to make sure, at the simplest level, that we are not making any mistakes.

But what about the example I used before, namely. "$2 + 2 = 4$"? In what sense could we possibly be deceived in this? What does "forgetting" mean in this context? It is true that there *can* be a temporal order to the thoughts composing "$2 + 2 = 4$". If we say it to ourselves this way: "Two plus two equals four," then of course the first saying of "two" will precede the second, and both will precede "four." But do we have to go through this temporal sequence to think "$2 + 2 = 4$"? Can we not just see that "$2 + 2 = 4$" with no temporal precedence involved?

To take an even simpler example, I visualize a triangle. It does not matter what kind of triangle it is. In this case do I not simply see that the triangle has three sides? One has to count, it is true, to find out if some regular figure is a chiliagon, but I do not have to count to three to see three of something. How is a doubt possible here? And if it is not possible, then why does Descartes suggest that it is? This question has both a philosophical and a rhetorical answer to it, and they are not mutually exclusive, but build upon one another.

Descartes was not a stupid man. There are clear indications that he is never very serious in his radical doubts about mathematics and geometry. The first knowledge he rehabilitates after the *cogito* is precisely mathematical and geometrical knowledge. It is also interesting that he never mentions logic *per se*. We never hear of the deceiving demon deceiving us into thinking that a proposition and its negation can both be true. Nor does Descartes suggest that we might be deceived by the meanings of the words we use, for he uses words to raise the question of doubt in the first place. Meanings are ideas in the mind and thus, for Descartes, incorrigible when severed from referential judgments. It is true that we sometimes use words without a clear understanding of their meaning, but when we achieve a clear understanding of them, certainty of meaning is attained.

It is a commonplace that to doubt at all requires something which is not doubted. There are many things about which the deceiving demon cannot create doubts. It is the *cogito* which Descartes stresses, because of his epistemological project of founding knowledge upon the principle of reason in the individual. The *cogito* gives us the certainty of our own minds and the ideas in them. Mathematics, geometry, and logic give us another kind of certainty. The crossing-point is mathematical physics, in which the mathematics plays an a priori role. For as he states,[24] we have in our mathematical descriptions of physical reality a perfectly well-formed and consistent system for describing the universe even if the universe as a system of physical objects does not exist. Descartes goes on to enlist the help of God to make the connection between our ideas and the external objects they represent, but mathematical physics already contains consistent means of describing these otherwise hypothetical objects.

What, then, is the deceiving demon doing in the *Meditations* if it has so many intrinsic problems? The deceiving demon is there like the devil in a fundamentalist sermon. He collects our fears and reflects them back to us enlarged and distorted. He forcefully shows us the pit of skepticism. On the other hand, if we look steadily at the deceiving demon, he gets smaller and smaller until he and our fears finally disappear.

· The deceiving demon is a rhetorical device with a philosophical point. It is there to instigate philosophical questioning. Descartes tries to put the fear of skepticism into the mind of the reader. He must make this fear vivid, concrete, and memorable. If Descartes can make the deceiving demon real for the reader, he will have gone a long way toward making his solution to the problem of skepticism real as well. He makes his philosophy of clear and distinct ideas seem relevant to a problem which the reader now feels. He first creates the illness which his philosophy is designed to cure. Once the reader has caught the bug, Dr Descartes' medicine can begin to work. At the very least he will succeed in opening the mind of the reader to a different approach to the nature of "investigation" and "thought."

Much the same effect is produced by Descartes' use of the metaphor, "Life is a dream." Perhaps life is but a dream and we merely dream our lives away. How can we know that we are not dreaming when we think we are awake? Is this really a serious philosophical problem? Serious philosophical solutions have certainly been given. One standard response is that the difference between dreaming and waking is provided by the coherence of our waking life as opposed to the incoherent and fragmentary nature of our dreams. According to this story, dreams have a logic of their own, but it is not the logic of our ordinary waking experience. It is this ordinary logic which helps Descartes to make the distinction between merely subjective experiences on the one hand, and objective ones on the other. Nevertheless, there is no definite criterion by which we may infallibly judge that we are not dreaming.

Suppose that by stipulation I dream in accordance with ordinary waking logic. In that case I will not be able to turn to the coherence of waking life to make the distinction between it and a dream. There will be nothing to distinguish one from the other. At least hypothetically, therefore, I can make the case for a dream which is indistinguishable from waking life. Nevertheless, if it really is a dream, then one big difference remains. In the voice of the story, the objects I encounter in dreams are not real. They have no objective existence outside of my own mind.

This points up a difficulty with the dream hypothesis. If there is no way in principle to exclude dreams which exactly mimic waking life; and if, in that case, there is no criterion for distinguishing them from waking life, it follows that we have no warrant to claim that it is, in fact, a dream at all. Without the contrast to waking life the concept of a dream loses all application. Simple analysis shows us that dreams are no threat to knowledge. They cannot subvert the distinction between waking and dreaming. No rational doubt comes of it.

The problems presented by dream phenomena, like those by the deceiving demon, fade away upon closer investigation. They are not able to withstand critical scrutiny. This is in perfect accord with our ordinary rejection of any such problem. If the problem persists, then the place to discuss it is a psychoanalyst's consulting room. A whole range of our activities and practices are carried out on the assumption that there is no problem about distinguishing between dreams and waking life. The doubt can only be theoretico-rhetorical, not practical. Even theoretically, as we saw, the doubt carries little conviction.

Descartes' doubt is called "methodological" to distinguish it from real doubts we might have about how things are in a particular case. This points to the rhetorical strategy involved in using an unreal doubt to further a new search for the foundations of human knowledge. The doubt generated by reflection upon dreams is philosophically inadequate, but a great rhetorical success. However, its rhetorical success is not philosophically neutral. There is no way to separate Descartes' philosophy and his philosophical writings. The indirect means he employs, without spelling them out, affect the way he is understood and how his philosophical practice is assimilated.

The rhetorical dimension of philosophy is audience-directed and adapted. It arises from the necessity of preparing the reader to think philosophically; in Descartes' case, to understand the issues and problems involved with skepticism and the search for certain knowledge. A beginning must be made by which someone is acclimatized to an unfamiliar mode of thought. The unreality of the doubt engendered by the dream metaphor and the story of the deceiving demon becomes transparent. In the story which

Descartes is telling, skeptical doubts are represented in the strongest fashion by the use of the strongest language and imagery. They are presented as real question marks hanging over our existence and perceptions.

The unsophisticated or novice reader may be shaken out of epistemological complacency by the fables of the deceiving demon and the dream. They serve to focus and intensify concerns about knowledge. Such concerns may have been absent. Descartes' stories and images serve to awaken or even create doubts by putting human weakness and fallibility in the strongest possible light. It does not matter that the stories and images which effect a change in our concerns will not stand up to rigorous philosophical criticism. They will have produced their philosophical effects.

Descartes' use of narrative techniques and imagery is rhetorical in the broadest sense. He is writing in the arena of persuasion. However, it is not rhetorical in the sense of practicing an ornate style to embellish an empty thought. It is a rhetorical need built into the exigencies of writing for a reader in the first place. Descartes' stories and images are part of a philosophical rhetoric designed to separate the reader from his or her connections with an external world and other people. Descartes' *Meditations* are exercises in isolation, and out of them is born a singular mind capable of self-reflection and not reliant upon external authority to justify its judgments.

Descartes' philosophical prose, though it eschews rhetoric in the name of rational transparency, is far from transparent itself. It is full of indirection. While saying that he only wishes for plain speaking and straightforward communication, he practices a highly advanced perlocutionary activity in his writing. Nor will we be able to count on Descartes to spell out his rhetorical strategy to us. We must look for his indirections by ourselves.

The deceiving demon and the question of dreams exist to sharpen our appetite for reason and clear objective thinking. By setting up the deceiving demon as the instigator of epistemological insecurity, Descartes is trying to get the reader to change mental gears and shift into a different mode of thought. This can only be a perlocutionary effect of Descartes' writing. It cannot be accomplished in the text, but only in the reader. By reading the texts the reader is persuaded to think another way, is startled, perhaps confused, moved, or otherwise affected by them. Descartes has managed to bring about these things in such a way that we still judge his writings to be relevant to present philosophical concerns. It may be that his dualism is finally incoherent, but he presents it in a forceful and memorable way. He accomplishes this through philosophical indirection, rhetoric, and perlocutionary action. The dream and the deceiving demon play their part.

Epistemological insecurity makes Descartes' search for certain foundations of knowledge an imperative for us as well as for him. He invites us to seek the truth with him, armed only with reason and clarity. Once we have found the *cogito* and found it secure against doubt, then we may be predisposed to follow him the rest of the way through his systematic philosophy. In any event, a persuasive text can never do more than to predispose the reader to come along the rest of the way. Dreams and deceiving demons are to tempt us into the thought which will liberate us from them both.

It is unclear whether Descartes intended to produce the effects which his writings have achieved. That he intended to have some effect upon his readers is clear through the highly rhetorical strategy which he adopts. We have seen it working through the deceiving demon and the dream. But it is important to remember that we are dealing here with indirect communication and the production of perlocutionary effects. These effects are not solely at the would-be producer's discretion. They transcend the producer's intentions. For example, I might try, but fail, to alarm you by saying, "Your house is burning down." You may hate your house and my remark may bring surprised delight as you think of the insurance money. There is always the risk of failure in perlocutionary action.

Another point to recall is that the failure to have the intention to produce a perlocutionary effect in a reader or hearer does not rule out the production of such effects. Not only can one try but fail to produce perlocutionary effects, one can also produce them without trying. It may be this way with Descartes. Fortunately, we do not have to decide the question here. We have Descartes' writings, and the writings on Descartes' writings. In them we find traces of Descartes' rhetorical strategy, and the effects produced or likely to be produced by them.

The difficulty with indirect communication is that there is no sure-fire conventional way to bring it off. Nevertheless, there are near-conventional ways to do it. For a politician in a nationalistic country, waving the flag is an almost sure way to bring patriotic citizens around to his or her way of thinking. Of course that does not work if the citizens no longer feel patriotic. The "near convention" fails to hold. The effectiveness of perlocutionary action depends very much on the context of the act.

All this is quite dubious from the point of view of a fundamentalist epistemology. Descartes does not wish to approach his subject indirectly if he can avoid it. He cannot avoid it, so he minimizes its impact by transcending it. The cultivation of reason and clear thinking brings us to the point at which we see through the stories and images by which we have approached the subject. Once we have the concept of a mathematical physics, we no longer need the doubts generated by the story of the dream and the deceiving demon. Once we have the means to make sense of the world as a self-contained physical universe, perhaps we no longer need the stories and images of Descartes' God to bolster knowledge. Skeptical doubts can make no practical headway.

There is a long tradition in philosophy of talk about different methods of attaining and expressing knowledge. Of these, there are some which have a double aspect. Plato called it the method of collection and division; Aristotle, dialectic; Descartes, analysis and synthesis. The way to knowledge is one thing, the way back another. What strikes us last in the order of learning turns out to be first in the order of being. We must start with whatever truth is at hand and work from there toward a more comprehensive vision. Once we have attained it, we can then present it systematically and analytically.

As stated, this distinction is too strong. The comprehensive vision must be expressed. We cannot isolate a philosophy and examine it in a vacuum. The truth is that in so far as philosophy is written or spoken, it has some connection with another, a reader or hearer. There is no philosophy in Descartes or anyone else which can be wholly abstracted from its persuasive context. For Descartes that means getting people to think for themselves as isolated individuals, to think philosophically. The deceiving demon and the dream doubts are means of bringing about these effects. They play an important role in starting up the game of rational enquiry which Descartes' philosophy promotes.

What these case studies have been designed to show is the

rhetorical context of philosophical writings. Whether or not the writings concerned indicate a willing or unwilling use of tropical language and persuasive strategies, all of them show evidence of perlocutionary action. Writings address an audience, and that audience must be taken into account. We will now examine more closely the concepts which will allow us to grasp more fully the nature of philosophical rhetoric and its pervasiveness in philosophical writings.

Chapter Three

INDIRECTION, PERLOCUTIONARY ACTION, AND RHETORIC

Among the connections between concepts established here are those which link the "art" of rhetoric with indirect communication and the production of perlocutionary effects. If we combine this with the thought that philosophy exists in uncertain and merely probable circumstances and speaks to an audience similarly situated, an inescapable philosophical rhetoric emerges. There are a number of possible attitudes to this fact. We will examine a few.

One attitude is expressed in the view that if there is a philosophical rhetoric, it is of negligible philosophical importance or use. It is mere window dressing. Style is one thing, content another. The thought remains the same even if the style of presentation is changed. That is because the properly philosophical content consists of necessary truths which never change. The discourse of the philosophers is of matters beyond the embrace of time and contingency.

Consider geometry. It is not necessary to accept Euclid's axioms, but if they are accepted, then his theorems follow necessarily. It is of secondary concern how someone is brought to grasp and accept the axioms. Geometrical rhetoric, if it exists at all, exists there. It is part of geometrical pedagogy. The truth of Euclid's theorems, given his axioms, lies outside the vicissitudes of educational practice. Perhaps we will have to modify our teaching of Euclid, and hence change our rhetoric, but not the substance of the teaching.

Since, presumably, what is true is so independently of what human beings might think or say about it, it will also be true independently of how anyone comes to learn it. The truth of a theorem of geometry does not seem to depend directly upon how I or anyone else come to learn about it. How we learn things most efficiently is a matter of educational psychology and has little or no philosophical interest.

Philosophy is like geometry. Both aim to achieve clear analyses, rigorous demonstrations, and rational syntheses. They both seek to show by stringent argument truths which transcend the particular beliefs and attitudes of the audience. Yet rhetoric applies just to such changeable items as these and thus drops out of philosophical consideration.

This, or something like it, is the view of someone who takes up the first attitude to the question of philosophical rhetoric. Though I will argue that it cannot be sustained, the argument is not a negligible one. It is as difficult to maintain that philosophical truth is, metaphorically speaking, geometrical, as it is to maintain that philosophical truth is wholly produced and determined by our interpretative schemata. This latter view rejects the concept of truth as an objective standard of judgment necessary to our use of language. Both views have something to contribute to our study of indirection in philosophical writings and practices, but neither alone is capable of giving a complete account.

My own view, which will emerge more fully in the course of the work, is that neither extreme can account for the dynamics of philosophical activity. Philosophy can approach geometry in its demands for clarity, precision, necessity, and universality. But it can also undermine those demands. To argue that philosophy has strict necessary and sufficient conditions for including or excluding putative samples of philosophical writing is to argue on the basis of suppressed premises. The mental standpoint which adopts conditions of inclusion does not, in the activity of inclusion or exclusion, question the basis of that very judgment. Part of the indirectness of philosophical writing is that it remains, and must remain to some degree, enthymematic in its own terms. The missing premise must be supplied by the audience. Like the blind spots in one's field of vision, the enthymemes of philosophical writing are obscured by their position in rhetorical strategies of persuasion.

This should not blind us, however, to the central role of truth in philosophical investigation. The temptation is to reduce philosophy to rhetoric once the vital connection between the two has been uncovered. This is an injustice to the way in which philosophical discourse is carried out. It is unjust even to the concept of truth as it is used rhetorically in philosophical writing.

If philosophers cease to claim that they are trying to say something true, what is the point of their speaking or writing at all? Philosophy collapses directly into rhetoric. What is true becomes simply what people can be persuaded to believe for as long as they can be persuaded to believe it. In so far as "truth" enters the language games of philosophy, it does so merely as a rhetorical counter.

This is an interesting hypothesis and it provides a fertile ground for exploration. Yet the appeal to truth in philosophy goes beyond its use as a rhetorical device. Philosophical speech and writing imply the existence of truths which transcend the beliefs and opinions of individual writers and readers, speakers and hearers. The paradoxical nature of the recent attempts to rid ourselves of the burdens of the search for truth in philosophy has simply resulted in a shift of the concept of truth, not in its abolition. It is paradoxical to write philosophy but to admit that everything one writes is false. It is possible to deny that the question of truth or falsity has a meaningful application. But in that case, surely, we have simply pushed the question of truth one step back. If one writes to undermine the concept of truth as traditionally conceived, another concept emerges to take its place. It will not look the same; different discursive moves will be allowed and disallowed; but its function in regulating the discussion will not change.

This attitude to the existence of philosophical rhetoric expresses itself in the denial that any truth transcends human subjectivity. We make our judgments about the world and other people, God and morality, art and creativity, and everything else through a web of concepts which prescribe the shapes truth can assume. We judge the world as we have the power to represent it to ourselves. This "representation" of the world in fact constructs it. Truth in all spheres belongs to this construction.

The problem with this reply is that it leaves philosophical writing without its *raison d'être*. If all truth is bound to our means of representing the world, then philosophical truths will also be. The advocates of philosophy will no longer be able to argue for the truth of views which transcend the beliefs and opinions of individual human beings. That is the end of philosophy as we know it. The rhetorical strategies of philosophical writing produce effects in learners/readers which predispose them to understand or reject various modes of thinking. Each mode carries with it its own paradigm of truth and intelligibility. But these standards are internal to the rhetorical projection of the whole work, and stand or fall by the success with which the learner/reader is brought around to a different way of thinking.

This answer brings with it a correspondingly different conception of the role of rhetoric in philosophy. No longer merely pedagogical, rhetoric provides us with the building blocks out of which our worlds are constructed. We cannot separate philosophy and the results of philosophical investigations from the learning of it. Learning what philosophers have said and written and learning to ask and discuss philosophical questions is part of what doing philosophy is. Since, according to this story, the world is a construction and nothing in-itself that we can know, shifts in conceptual schemes will produce other constructions. Coming to understand what philosophy is, is coming to be able to do it. Each insight and advance in understanding implies, at the same time, an increase in the ability to reflect upon the world from one philosophical standpoint or another. The first step to understanding philosophy is also a philosophical step, and there is no point at which the one who learns is not doing philosophy, nor is there an end to the doing of it.

Philosophy becomes an endless conversation.[1] It becomes polyphonic. The authority of the "authorities" is broken. We can discuss philosophical issues to our heart's content, but there will never be a resolution of radically contrasting world-constructions. The dialogue can be interesting or boring, but a truth which resides outside of the contrasting world-constructions is not conceivable. Nevertheless, the exploration of their differences gives us an insight into the gulfs which separate different ways of thinking about and experiencing the world.

The danger which some would see in the idea that philosophy is conversation is connected with the fear of seeing philosophy collapse into rhetoric, the fear that all philosophical arguments remain in the arena of the probable. If that is true, then they also remain in the arena of the rhetorical. Philosophy would become a kind of epideictic oratory, in which the pleasures of a good conversation are the point of the activity. For example, the question is not whether foundationalism or anti-foundationalism in epistemology is true, but how well the case is put. The best we can do is convince an audience of the truth of the case we are putting, and as we have seen, the verdict is up to the audience, not to the speaker or writer alone. "To convince" is not an illocutionary verb, and there are no transparent, straightforward means of bringing conviction about. It will depend partly upon the skill and timing of those seeking to convince and partly upon the reaction of the audience, since how an audience reacts will be a function of its own perceptions and means of interpreting the signs.

Philosophical writing contains a hermeneutic strategy which indirectly displays itself in the text through its rhetoric. The text invites a reader, as it were, to interpret it in certain ways. This is an invitation which can be ignored or refused, but must be noticed to be refused. Rhetorical devices induce the reader to apply particular interpretative schemata to the text. If the reader accepts the invitation, then the text will make sense, the sense imposed upon it by the interpretative schemata themselves. If not, then some very strange readings emerge which break the rhetorical project of the whole.

The fact that varying readings can be given to the same text shows the independence of the reader from its rhetorical strategy. It points up the perlocutionary nature of the effects produced. The reader can construct or deconstruct a meaning, can go along or decide not to go along with the internal hermeneutic of the text. Many examples of this are found in the writings of the "literary" theorists. I will mention one oft-cited example from the literature of literary theory [2], and then explore the possibility of doing the same thing to a philosophical text.

The text is Jules Verne's *Mysterious Island*. The story that is told of it runs like this: the text of *Mysteriours Island* is, on the surface, a vindication of the dominant values of an imperial capitalism. The "Island" is the Third World. It is a world completely plastic and amenable to colonizers. The natives know their place and live in happy servitude. The colonizers "improve" the land, start up an economy, and bring civilization to benighted areas of the globe. This is the officially optimistic side of Verne's tale.

The dark side has Captain Nemo lurking about in his submarine beneath the island. The connection between the ostensible reality of order and production on the one hand and Captain Nemo on the other is completely adventitious. What it shows is that the conscious or explicit ideology of the text is torn in various places. When we look closely it turns out that all is not well with triumphant colonialism. The underside consists of dark and mysterious forces, such as Captain Nemo, because the conscious ideology of the text is blocked in its understanding of what is really wrong. Verne registers an unease at the heart of the colonial project, but cannot quite make out what it is. Nemo does not fit, but he is there.

The moral of this story is that Verne's text works against its own rhetorical grain. Something keeps upsetting paradise. My question now is whether the same might not hold for some philosophical texts and philosophical writing. If it does, we have good evidence that readers have some independence from the rhetorical devices and strategies we discover in philosophical writing.

The text I have chosen is A.J. Ayer's *Language, Truth, and Logic*.[3] This may seem a strange choice. After all, it is hard to think of a book which is more blatantly anti-rhetorical in its posture. The thesis of the book is that philosophy has nothing to state on its own behalf. Its job is merely to analyze concepts, not to put forward positive theories. When Ayer spots a philosopher who speaks a speculative and metaphorical language, he attacks immediately. His book is highly polemical and recognized to be so. Ayer's treatment of Hegel's Absolute is one example. He takes the short way of ridicule and dismissal, rather than the long one of detailed discussion.

Let us turn to the setting in which Ayer enunciates his position. According to the regular story, Ayer is bringing logical positivism to an English philosophical audience. One reason we find an adversarial stance in Ayer is that the philosophical climate of the day still felt the influence of German Idealism, and especially Hegel. Ayer must make himself heard against the background hum of speculative discourse.

Ayer says it is a young man's book, full of vim and vigor. His position emerges with a nakedness later covered over with qualifications. We note that in later editions of his text, Ayer spends an increasing amount of time qualifying and defending his initial formulation of the verification principle in the face of "misinterpretations" and objections. The irony is that the point of the initial formulation is precisely to arouse strong reactions, not to lose the reader in abstractions and sophisticated argument. That can come later after interest has been aroused. Ayer's job is to arouse that interest in the first place. The "misinterpretations" of the text had to be produced first before it became worth while to answer any questions in detail. Once he had established logical positivism on the philosophical scene, he went on to make a career out of defending and modifying his initial position.

Language, Truth and Logic is an act of establishment which relies on the securing of perlocutionary effects. These, as we have seen, are in part dependent upon the audience and its "interpretation" ("misinterpretation") of the text. Therefore, though the argument of the text is explicitly on the side of straightforward linguistic communication and rules out the meaningfulness of rhetoric in our descriptions of the world as observed, the work itself employs a strong philosophical rhetoric.

This irony emerges clearly in connection with a familiar objection to the principle of verification. The principle itself is not verifiable, and hence possesses no literal significance. It is glaringly obvious that this fact undercuts the rhetorical drift of the argument which excludes meaning from statements which are not, even in principle, verifiable. How could such a distressingly obvious objection escape even the young and impetuous Ayer?

The answer to this question can be found in the rhetorical nature of the first formulation of the verification principle. Though it contains logical problems, it is none the less vivid and memorable, and has controversial implications. Though admittedly wrong-headed, the first formulation had a punch which none of the subsequent formulations has had. It hit the idealist antagonist where it hurt the most, right at the heart of speculative metaphysics. Yet the option is there, for an idealist who spots the paradox in the verification principle, to deflect the attack if forearmed with irony. The perlocutionary effects of the text, in that case, are other than those which the overt rhetorical program encourages.

On the other hand, the vividness of the principle, the way it made philosophy cut and dried and guarded it against idle rhetorical chat, did produce a clear-cut and seemingly arguable position from which to question received philosophical wisdom. It was a young man's book designed for a young and rebellious audience. And though it was ostensibly aimed at any sort of speculative philosophy, its arguments are at the disposal of anyone

69

whose attitudes to philosophical activity are first channeled and shaped by the conscious rhetorical project of Ayer's text.

Logical positivism is as much a mood, a philosophical temperament, or an attitude as it is a straightforward philosophical theory. It is as much an orientation as a doctrine. *Language, Truth and Logic* is hard on soft-headed philosophical thinking. We must at all times be clear what we are saying and what we can say. Outside of that we should either become poets or shut up. Ayer has more respect for poets than erring philosophers because at least the poets admit that they are dealers in dreams and not realities. (If any do make such claims, they should be tarred with the same brush as the philosophers.)

The philosophical rhetoric of Ayer's text works towards changing the attitudes of readers whose resistance to logical positivism must be overcome, or to strengthening attitudes already in accord with the overt project of philosophical analysis found in it. But, in a typically rhetorical fashion, indirect means are employed to bring the reader round to the mental stance in which, the verification principle say, makes obvious sense. For the purposes of bringing people around to this point of view, the vivid, though faulty, formulation of the principle is the most apt.

Thus it does not matter whether or not Ayer saw the weaknesses in the verification principle. What mattered was the insertion of logical positivism into the philosophical arena and on to the agenda of philosophical debate. Though Ayer may have been aware of the difficulties raised by the first formulation of his principle, he may still have chosen it for its rhetorical and yet philosophical effects. Ayer wants to push for analysis as *the* method of philosophy. He wants the audience to react in certain ways. In the wider rhetorical context the fact that the verification principle is without literal meaning in its own terms does not affect the ability of the theory to produce its perlocutionary effects. The principle does not need to be literally meaningful to have persuasive force.

This case is similar to that of Descartes' deceiving demon and the question of the dream (see pp. 57–8). We saw there that the devices Descartes uses will not stand up well to detailed questioning. Nevertheless, they are effective tools in the production of suitable perlocutionary effects in the audience. The verifiability principle does not stand up to close questioning any better than

Descartes' demon, yet it, too, is an effective way to launch a kind of philosophical discourse which remains discussed even when much of the import of its philosophy has been rejected.

If my account of the rhetoric of *Language, Truth and Logic* is correct, then we can see A.J. Ayer as the Jules Verne of philosophy. The mysterious island is a philosophical Third World populated by natives steeped in idealism. Logical positivism has come to exercise benign rule over the natives who gladly accept it. The natives who persist in speaking nonsense will simply be counted among the poets. The serious and literal use of language will be set against deviant speech or writing.

But there is a Captain Nemo in the form of a mysterious disruption of the main message of the text, and that is the very principle of the literally meaningful use of language upon which it rests. This produces a nagging suspicion that all is not well with the theory. Yet it is perfectly possible to approach meaning in the way it suggests without worrying too much about the problem. Anxiety over the verifiability theory of meaning has never prevented anyone from adopting logical positivism as a program of philosophical investigation. The faulty principle works to incite the reader to engage in philosophical analysis, to develop a certain taste for hard-headed and unsentimental thinking, and a readiness to uncover and denounce slipshod and woolly thinking wherever it may be found, but especially in religion and metaphysics.

This optimistic and combative attitude is fostered by the philosophical rhetoric of the text, and yet disrupted by it through the faulty principle. It comes as a surprise that it should be faulty at all. What is this problem with the principle that it should come to plague us, while at the same time working so well elsewhere? Its relation to the plot of *Language, Truth and Logic* is like that of Nemo to the plot of *Mysterious Island*; namely, a purely adventitious one, otherwise unconnected with it. But it produces anxiety about the main program.

The result is that it is still possible to be a combative positivist, but the optimism is harder to maintain. The rhetoric of *Language, Truth and Logic* simply does not have the same punch today as when it first appeared. The audience has changed and so has the philosophical climate. It is perhaps easier today than when it first came out to spot the rhetoric of Ayer's text, now that the issues which first fired the enthusiasm for logical positivism have cooled.

The verifiability principle, like the deceiving demon, works indirectly through the text to change or reinforce the thought patterns of the audience. It works best on those to whom it is addressed, an audience which possesses or can develop the requisite perspective.

Ayer's text invites collusion. The reader is addressed as someone possessing eminent good sense, someone who is not a fool, not gullible, superstitious, or easily taken in. For someone like that, the overt line of *Language, Truth and Logic* will seem to be the obvious course to take despite reservations about the details of the argument. If the reader is not someone like that, then the text invites him or her to become sensible. The text acts as an invitation to play a game, the game of being sensible. It invites the reader to play a role and see what comes out of it. Whether the text succeeds in making someone sensible, or merely enables the reader to pretend to be sensible for the sake of argument, the result is a success for Ayer's official philosophical rhetoric. In either case the reader can now go on to work out the further implications of the explicit philosophical direction of the writing.

One of the main jobs of philosophical rhetoric is to orientate the audience/reader in philosophical space through a process of exclusion. *Language, Truth and Logic* does this by reducing the field of possible philosophical discourse. This bracing simplification of the job of philosophy has impact, however, only in a mind prepared to take it on board and entertain it. The taking up of a philosophical position cannot be separated from the taking up of a rhetorical stance as well. The mind-set of the reader who can embrace logical positivism has certain features which include a no-nonsense attitude to philosophical thought.

These are some of the perlocutionary effects the main line of text gives out. But as we have seen, all is not well. The suspicion remains that the text practices a disguised metaphysics of a perfectly objectionable kind. We might say that Ayer's philosophical rhetoric breaks ranks with itself at this point. There is a counter-rhetoric in the same text which is blind to its own existence, for otherwise the refreshing, though naive, force of the main argument is vitiated. The depth of insight the theory affords in one narrow focus is paid for by the loss of peripheral vision.

Our examination of *Language, Truth and Logic* has shown the impossibility of completely severing philosophy from rhetoric. It is also wrong-headed simply to allow philosophy to collapse into a rhetoric purged of philosophical interest. Those have been the two attitudes toward philosophical rhetoric we have investigated so far. Is there another attitude possible? There is, but it involves holding in mind a distinction which is alternately constructed and dismantled. It is perfectly possible to distinguish philosophy from rhetoric, but that does not mean we can conceive of either one of them without the other. They are different but bound to one another. We forget this point at our peril.

If we forget philosophy's links with rhetoric we are liable to fly off into such abstract and highly sophisticated reasoning that we soon lose touch with all but a tiny specialist audience. Hence, it will appear non-rhetorical, but only because of shared though unspoken assumptions which inform their common practice. For example, if we consider the considerable literature on the problem of counter-factuals, we find writing which does not appear rhetorical in the least. There are fairly polite exchanges in the learned journals in which critical views are aired. There are disagreements about interpretation, analysis, and logic. But the whole discussion is nevertheless covertly rhetorical.

This once again raises the question of the philosopher's audience. People who publish articles in the learned journals are addressing or designating their audiences in advance. They are people, like the writer, who think about the kinds of topics raised in the journal. It is a commonplace that different journals have different editorial policies. A piece which might find a publisher in a journal devoted to phenomenology might not find one in a journal devoted to logical analysis. The very act of sending off a text for publication already takes a prospective readership into consideration. Editorial selection is rhetorical. Editorial policy selects for the enthymemes embedded in the policy itself.

The fact that the writer writes for an audience or readership places his contribution solidly within a rhetorical context. Rhetoric is simply the arena of persuasive argument. A glance at the established philosophical journals is enough to show that much of the material refers to previous discussion of one issue or another. We find A's article on B's response to C's seminal article on X. We find straightforward replies as well as defences and criticisms of different positions.

To write for a journal is to commit oneself to a certain familiarity with the current work being done and considered worth doing. It is also to commit oneself to a way of doing philosophy and the commonplaces which inform it. Since to write is to write for someone, the question always arises of how to make some kind of impression or impact on the audience. The illusion of a philosophical space free of rhetoric is the result of forgetfulness. No special effort is made to arouse our interest in the topic at hand because it is assumed that anyone who picks up the journal will already be interested in its contents. The specialized journals, therefore, appear free of rhetoric. However, the rhetoric has not vanished but has simply gone underground.

We must try to think of rhetoric and philosophy as going together, but separately. We ought, in philosophy, to maintain our search for a truth which transcends the current opinions of proponents or detractors while realizing the inherently rhetorical arena in which philosophical investigation is carried out. Philosophical writing is persuasive writing, but a persuasive writing which aims at a truth which transcends both writers and readers. This is not to say that we can know when we have attained this truth, but only that we aim for it. Truth is not a property which inheres in propositions, but lies instead in the direction of philosophical inquiry. The inquiry is orientated toward the truth.

This may become clearer by way of an analogy with Kant's distinction between the noumenal and the phenomenal world.[4] We recall that in the familiar story of Kant's distinction we are able to call to our service a certain double vision. We can understand the human being as part of a natural order of cause and effect, completely determined in every respect. We can also think of the human being as a moral agent, free to choose to do or not to do what morality requires. A double description of a human being now becomes possible. On the one hand, we have the description of a human being as a natural being, acting in accordance with the laws of its nature. On the other hand, we have the description of an autonomous and free rational agent who is responsible for his or her actions and words, and acts from a rational principle.

Both descriptions apply to human beings under different aspects. Kant maintains that they are compatible with one another. It is somehow the same being which is both empirical and moral. One description belongs to the phenomenal world, one to the noumenal.

There is no chance that one will obstruct the other for their paths never cross.

We can describe philosophical writing in two ways as well. The phenomenal side of philosophy is its rhetoric. It is what appears in the text. Deceiving demons, waking dreams, verifiability principles are all phenomena of the text. We can pick them out for special mention or investigation. The noumenal side is the realm of truth and reasoned argument. Thus we can look at philosophy writing in two ways. First, we can look at it as rhetoric, then as straightforward argument. It is a bit like Wittgenstein's famous duck-rabbit.[5] Now you see it as a duck, now as a rabbit, but you cannot see the duck and the rabbit at the same time. The connections between philosophy and rhetoric are indirect. They relate philosophical argument to strategies of perlocutionary action.

We can examine philosophical writing with an eye to its rhetorical strategies, devices, and images. This is in large part what I am doing in this book. But it is equally feasible to discuss arguments in the rhetorical situation one finds oneself in, according to the local rules, which still require us to speak about what is true, about what goes beyond current interests and opinions. Just as we can describe a human being as part of nature and still ascribe to him or her a moral life, so we can describe philosophical writings as rhetoric or as argumentation. Both are applicable, both belong to the terms of philosophical rhetoric. In the western tradition the emphasis has been on argumentation and logic, not rhetoric. The two sides have been opposed and ranked hierarchically with logic and argumentation on top. In this climate it is a necessary corrective to emphasize the other side. In doing this, however, we should not forget that philosophical writing is as much about logic and argument as it is about rhetorical techniques of persuasion.

Good arguments are seen to be good only from a point of view. Philosophical rhetoric works to create the point of view from which the arguments will be seen to be good. Once that is achieved we can judge the arguments on their own merits, for we shall then agree in general about what will count as a good argument and what a bad one. These are the commonplaces that go without saying when we evaluate arguments.

Philosophers can still investigate the truth of philosophical views, the strengths and weaknesses of different kinds of philosophical argument, and the examples set out for discussion. Under this description rhetoric has not disappeared but it is no longer the focus of attention. We can also attend to the argument and describe philosophy in this way. We can enter the debate about what is true and not give much explicit attention to rhetoric or the rhetorical situation. My point is that we ought to be able to do both.

A Derridean deconstruction of the dichotomy of philosophy and rhetoric would, I imagine, create the thought of an "archi-rhetoric" in which both "philosophy" and "rhetoric" are merely moments. One story of such a deconstruction goes like this.

There is no distinction between philosophy and rhetoric until philosophy establishes one to its own advantage. Plato's assessment of rhetoric and the character of the rhetor in the *Gorgias* is set up to prejudice the reader against rhetoric and for philosophy. Socrates makes it uncomfortable to contemplate "being an orator" or "being a sophist." Socrates makes one feel that there is something shameful in these occupations. This is not surprising, since Socrates argues that rhetoric is a kind of pandering and the rhetor a kind of pander. The rhetorician, on this account, is out to persuade an audience of something advantageous to himself with few scruples as to how the desired end is brought about.

Since what is important to the rhetor is success in the assembly or in the courts, and the job is to sway numbers of people at once, rhetoric functions and is evaluated only on that plane. If bringing on weeping members of one's family helps to sway the jury to mercy, it is a good rhetorical move. But something can be a good rhetorical move without being either good or for the good. This, at least, is Plato's position in the *Gorgias*. Rather than aim at truth which is difficult and requires concentration, the rhetor aims at pleasure, a coin of more common currency.

Socrates makes the rhetor out to be a low-life character who ekes a shady living out of persuasive talk unrelated to truth. So we clearly have an opposition between philosophy and rhetoric in which moral authority is vested in philosophy. The point is reached in the *Gorgias*[6] where Socrates claims that the only good of rhetoric is to make oneself eloquent in self-condemnation, to make a persuasive confession of one's own injustice.

This story continues with the observation that philosophy establishes itself by distinguishing itself from the other, in this case rhetoric. Yet upon closer investigation we discover that this act of distinguishing between philosophy and rhetoric is itself a rhetorical act. So it turns out that far from avoiding the taint of rhetoric, philosophy is itself a kind of rhetoric, call it "archi-rhetoric." In this way we explore the pretensions of a philosophy which would set itself outside the bounds of discourse.

It is not necessary to reiterate Derrida's views on logocentrism and the philosophy of presence.[7] Needless to say, the pretensions to truth in philosophy are exploded. For the truth which guides or directs philosophical investigation lies outside discourse, and that is not an option for us. Perhaps an "archi-rhetoric" is also an "archi-philosophy."

A Derridean deconstruction of philosophy has lessons for philosophers such as myself who do not wish to give up the goal of truth and intelligibility in philosophy. The deconstructive answer is like the one just discussed, which collapses philosophy and rhetoric, in opposition to the first which irrevocably severs the links between them. A just conception of philosophical rhetoric recollects the relations between philosophy and rhetoric without reducing one to the other or excluding one in favor of the other. My Derridean story is too reductive. Though it is true that philosophy is established as a separate activity by distinguishing itself from others, the distinction is not merely rhetorical, but also conceptual.

For example, when Plato distinguishes philosophy from rhetoric in the *Gorgias*, it is the interests of philosophy which are served. These are perlocutionary interests, interests which involve the reaction of an audience or reader. It is part of Plato's philosophical rhetoric that, in comparison to rhetoric, philosophy appears sublime. Plato has to motivate an audience to value reason (*logos*), dialogue, and rational persuasion. The task of motivating an audience is perlocutionary and hence relies on indirect, rhetorical means. "I motivate you to value rationality" is not a straightforward illocutionary act which depends merely upon "securing uptake" (capturing attention) and the possession of general linguistic abilities.

The problem is one of audience motivation. A perlocutionary act depends crucially upon the response of the audience. A conscious perlocutionary project involves judging one's audience and the likely means of winning it over. We are incited by Plato's words to take a humorous and yet pitying attitude toward sophists and orators. We are invited to understand that they do not know what they are saying but are speaking merely to secure their own advantage regardless of the merits of the case. We are invited to see ourselves, on the other hand, as superior to them, as the allies of Plato and Socrates.

Plato works, through Socrates, to bring about perlocutionary effects in the audience which run along the grain of his philosophical rhetoric. We start by realizing our own ignorance of "what is." From there we begin to ask questions about "what is." In the process we learn that "what is" must fit various criteria. Being alone is outside of space and time, outside of all chance and change. We learn the acceptable form of the answer to a "what is" question. No answer will suffice which is cast in the language of history and development. "What is" does not develop, since to develop implies a lack of being.

A distinction Plato often makes is that between "being" and "becoming." Rhetoric comes to be unflatteringly associated with "becoming." This is the world of change, decay, and history from which nothing of enduring value can be extracted. Another distinction, that between body and soul, associates rhetoric with the body, with similar distressing results. The rhetor panders to the pleasures and pains, hopes, fears, and other irrationalities of the audience. Pleasure itself is closely associated with the body, and it is bodily pleasure for the most part which the temperate human being controls.

All along the line of weighted oppositions rhetoric is associated with the lower of the two. In the opposition philosophy/poetry, for example, poetry is silent on the question of its own *logos*. Neither poets nor critics can give an account of poetry. The meaning of poems is hidden, despite commentary and criticism. The poem is silent and cannot speak its own reason.

Rhetoric is closely allied to poetry. Under "style" in rhetoric, for example, we find the poetic tropes, figures of speech and thought which form the basis of "poetic" writing. The major difference seems to be that while poetry aims to please and perhaps instruct,[8] rhetoric aims at the production of practical results. This is clearest, of course, in deliberative or judicial rhetoric. It is rather in ceremonial or epideictic oratory, suitable for serving up toasts at formal dinners, that rhetoric comes closest to poetry. Yet even here rhetoric operates in a public context which is also a moral one. For example, we can expect that a speech given in honor of a charitable donor will underline his or her goodness of character and exemplary role in the community. Much poetry is also epideictic, and situates its subject in a moral context of praise or blame.

In the analogy of the line,[9] both poetry and rhetoric occupy a position somewhere below the line. Rhetoric is tarred with the brush of poetry and they bring each other down. Everywhere we look there seems to be a way to link the philosophy/rhetoric distinction to the system of weighted oppositions which run like a backbone through the Platonic corpus. Derrida's contribution has been to take an X-ray as it were, of this corpus and to expose its backbone.

What this X-ray exposes is a vital link between rhetoric and philosophy in which the very descriptive language that Plato uses prejudices the case in favor of philosophy. However, it is important to recognize this fact without ruling out the possibility of the continuation of recognizable philosophical inquiry. A heightened awareness of the rhetorical setting of philosophical discourse need not lead to the conclusion that philosophy is just rhetoric, or even archi-rhetoric. Plato's unequal oppositions play a large part in his perlocutionary argument. It is by the use of oppositions and hierarchies that philosophy and the divine world of the Forms are highlighted before an audience. It is through their auspices that the audience is invited to the feast of philosophy. This is indeed rhetoric, but it is a philosophical rhetoric and not merely an instrumental one.

Philosophical rhetoric is not the rhetoric taught in the schools. It is not caught in the pages of rhetorical handbooks or constituted by sets of rhetorical devices. One of the main points about rhetoric in all its forms is its "timeliness." Plato must make his points about eternity in a "timely" way. The strong divisions in his thought between what is noble and what is base make for vivid and memorable images and give his thought passion. He is trying to move us toward thinking for ourselves in dialogue with others. Derrida reveals to us the way Plato does this, makes us conscious of his philosophical rhetoric.

For example, in the *Phaedrus* Plato has Socrates tell a myth in which the whole project of writing is rejected as "bad memory".[10] Yet Plato writes. Socrates inveighs against rhetoric yet Plato makes him a master of it. He knows how to use rhetoric for philosophical purposes. Socrates' famous irony, his gags, and word-play engage the reader on many levels of understanding and reaction. Plato is working on his audience in a complex fashion, but he is doing so from behind the scenes, indirectly. It is for the reader to "catch on" (recollect) or not.

The effects produced in an audience by a text depend in large part upon the audience itself. Plato's oppositions do not work on the "Derrida" of my story. He sees through them to their rhetorical basis. And that is really the end of the story. However, from the standpoint I wish to develop, it is not the end of the story. We can take in and assimilate all of this and still carry on doing philosophy. We can still argue about theories and points of view, assess the validity of arguments and all the rest of it. However, the philosopher's consciousness of what is involved in "doing philosophy" is altered.

What my "Derrida" notices is that while the grain of Plato's philosophical rhetoric heads in the direction of philosophy, not rhetoric, there is also an across-the-grain rhetoric in Plato's writing which subverts the advertized view. Plato writes. Sometimes he writes what can only be called poetry. He undoubtedly uses every rhetorical trick in the book. All of these activities miss the mark if Plato's advertized program of philosophy goes through. What, then, is the status of Plato's philosophical writing?

Plato's writing is persuasive writing, but it is also philosophy. There are many uncertainties but the philosophical ideals of rational inquiry and dialogue remain intact. To succumb to Plato's philosophical rhetoric is to become susceptible to logical argument. It is to come to distance oneself from daily life and the "timely" world of practical action. Plato's philosophical rhetoric clears a space in the reader's life for contemplation of the world outside the daily round.

This is one effect that nearly all decent philosophical writing produces. Even Derrida's own writings act out their complicated dance on a space inscribed within the everyday world of human existence. Any attempt to read his writing will be sufficient to convince the reader that here is a very complicated and demanding work. And what it demands is precisely that the reader forgo his or her "pre-Derridean" inclinations and prejudices and move in a different direction. The unwary reader cannot possibly find a way into the Derridean maze except by putting off the old Adam and putting on the new archi-Adam.

This need to move the reader to a different standpoint is also the need for philosophical rhetoric. Derrida uses the old distinctions to overcome or deconstruct them, but he puts others in their place. Western metaphysics erred, and that error has provided Derrida with the material to work with. What can deconstruction do without it? The move from philosophy/rhetoric to archi-rhetoric leaves philosophy in the position of commentator on its own productions; nothing remains for philosophy but an inexorable web of intertextual significations. This view is too pessimistic.

It may be true, as many have alleged, that there is little or no progress in philosophy. Progress is measured as an advance to some sort of goal or end. If the goal or end of philosophy is truth, then the lack of progress seems to put that end out of our reach. We cannot even measure how close we come to it, since we do not know what the truth is. Therefore, it is vain to speak of progress here. Is logical positivism an advance upon idealism? Do recent developments in logical techniques render all previous philosophy obsolete? There have been arguments produced to support positive answers to these questions. But as we have seen, my "Derrida" supports negative conclusions. In fact neither will do.

To return to Plato, we see that his philosophy and his rhetoric are bound together in what I've been calling his philosophical rhetoric. The fact that they are found together and are inseparable does not imply that Plato's philosophy cannot be discussed to some profit either in its own terms or in terms which make his philosophy relevant to us. The aim of possessing a truth, which is never actually realized in the Platonic corpus, is nevertheless vital to his philosophical argument.

Truth is the *topos* of philosophy, the place from which argument is produced and tested. It is also part of its rhetoric. The aim and concept of truth are necessary conditions for the possibility of philosophical investigation. On the one hand, it is the aim of such an investigation to arrive at the truth. On the other hand, it is the bar which any theory or philosophical position must pass in order to be accepted. Without the concept and aim of truth, philosophy degenerates into a simple struggle of beliefs and opinions which lacks a direction and a test of worthiness.

One way of reaching the "truth" in a rhetorical situation is for one or other of the opposing speakers or writers to throw in the towel, and recognize and concede his own errors. The other more common and likely end is a stand-off. Both sides maintain their positions in the face of critical objections and each attacks the other side in turn. Both sides of a philosophical dispute will maintain that truth is on its side, but will be unwilling to recognize the other's marks of truth and sound argument. Despite this, it is only in terms of truth that even this sort of discussion can go on. We can only agree to disagree with each other if we share an understanding of what truth should be, but disagree about what it is. The problem here is a blind spot in both parties which prevents either one of them from seeing its own presuppositions or recognizing its own rhetoric.

The fact that the opposition quickly seizes precisely upon the rhetoric of the proffered view is small consolation for those who suppose that they are simply speaking the truth. Those who fundamentally disagree with each other about philosophical questions will also disagree in their philosophical rhetoric. The grain of the rhetoric will invite the reader to adopt a certain stance and attitude from which the world looks different from how it did before. We can deconstruct philosophical positions if we wish, but we can also pursue philosophical questions as one who inquires. Both are possible.

Kant may help us again in this question of truth. My proposal is similar to the Kantian one of recommending truth as an ideal of reason.[11] It can be found not in the phenomena, in the texts, but in a regulative principle of the understanding. Kant, of course, held that the ideal of truth represents the possession of complete and total knowledge. This is the direction which inquiry must take, though it has no assurance that it will ever terminate. For us knowledge can only be fragmented and limited, but our drive is to overcome these limits and push on toward a unified knowledge. However much we may strive to attain it, complete unconditional knowledge is beyond our reach. Hence, truth is an ideal of reason and not a constitutive principle of the understanding.

I look at this matter in a way which side-steps the question of the unification of knowledge. Truth is a regulative principle of inquiry in general. But it is regulative not in the sense of driving on toward unity, but in the sense that it appeals to a state of affairs which exists independently of the proponents and detractors of different views. To discuss and enquire about the nature of things requires the concept of a truth which transcends the inescapably rhetorical setting in which all debate occurs. Truth is an ideal of rational discourse because our appeal to it transcends the rhetoric at our disposal. This same ideal is also rhetorical, for it plays its role in "timely" debates as the philosophical *topos par excellence.*

What it comes down to is this. We must understand the connection between philosophy and rhetoric as a dialectical one. There is no statement addressed to an audience which does not have a rhetorical or perlocutionary force. Nevertheless, the rhetoric in philosophical writing can be used, and is used, against rhetoric itself. This fact reveals a tension between philosophy and rhetoric, and it is this tension that I want to capture through a dialectical understanding of the relation of philosophy to rhetoric. However, this dialectic differs from that of Plato and that of Hegel.

It differs from Plato for it surrenders the goal of absolute knowledge of the Forms. It differs from Hegel because it does not propose an ultimate and purely conceptual grasp of the Whole. In other words, in my view the ends or directions created from the tensions between philosophy and rhetoric are local and historically generated, rather than absolutely universal and necessary. There is a movement of thought, not without its own logic, which we must situate within a historically produced arena of process and action; in other words, a rhetorical arena.

Let us explore this question by considering a current, rhetorically hot topic in philosophy: the question of "foundations" in epistemology. It is helpful to situate this question in its historical setting. A rough overview will do. There are three stages or periods worthy of note. The first period is a rhetorical period; the second, anti-rhetorical; and the third, rhetorical again, but with different themes from before. This three-part program of response is capable of expansion in either direction, but I want to locate and stress the period preceding the advent of mathematical physics, the one which triumphs with Newton and the Enlightenment, and the one born out of the dissatisfaction with the rule of reason.

In a world of change we must act without certain knowledge. We learn from experience the principles of our choices and actions. What matters here is not so much our knowledge but our ability to make the right decisions at the right time and place. Our actions reflect our understanding of the situation we find ourselves in. We live in the world of the probable, not in one of logical necessity. What matters in this world is the possession of "eloquence," of the ability to move people in directions they would not choose for themselves. But this must be done in ignorance of how things will turn out. If alternative verdicts can be rendered in a court, or alternative policies adopted in a political context, then the choice of one alternative will not rule out the possibility that the other is the better. A man may be convicted of murder in a perfectly legal manner and still be innocent. The adoption of a political policy might turn out to lead to disastrous consequences.

A good example of the latter is a story related by Thucydides in his history of the Peloponnesian War. Athens and Sparta are in the midst of a temporary truce. It is debated what to do. On the grounds of an encircling strategy it is proposed to send an expeditionary force to capture Sicily as a base of operations from which to attack Sparta from the west. Alcibiades speaks for the expedition; Nikias, an undefeated general, speaks for caution. As we know, Alcibiades carried the day, and the result was total disaster for the Athenians. Nikias had the better judgment. However, history alone can tell us the outcome. On the day there was no telling which way the course of events would go. There were only the differing opinions about the best course to take. In the absence of certain knowledge we must use every available means of persuasion to press the course of action we take to be the best.

What makes rhetoric so important in cases like this is the absence of knowledge of what the future will bring. Where the future is concerned we make the best plans we can devise and then see what happens. The crucial point for rhetoric is that in its arena the world is shaped to the word, since what will be is, in part, shaped by our decisions and actions. These are the very states of affairs which rhetoric works most effectively to bring about through persuasion. It is true, after all, that rhetoric involves a certain ignorance of what is the case, but this fact points to the irreducibly contingent field in which it operates.

With the rise of mathematical science the story changes considerably. It now becomes possible to think that knowledge can be attained through method, something anyone can acquire with the right training in analytical thought. We no longer have to put up with the uncertainties which plague the rhetorical arena. We no longer have to go by what we find most convincingly put forward. There is solid evidence now which no amount of smooth talking can gloss over. In a nutshell, we do not have to rely upon rhetoric to put forward, defend, or criticize scientific theories. Rhetoric is reduced to the merely ornamental trappings of truths better expressed plainly and without frills. Let the facts and formulae speak for themselves. For our part, let us but observe distinctly and think clearly, eschew the uncertainties of human life and concentrate on the great system of nature.

Talk about foundations in epistemology begins here. It enters through the metaphor of building. Rather than rely on what the ancients said to make our speech copious and eloquent, we should think for ourselves and be answerable to reason alone. The result is a building of knowledge which rests on a secure foundation. Different philosophers in the anti-rhetorical era had different ideas about what the building of knowledge rests on and what the building materials are.

The guiding thought is that knowledge must be beyond doubt, beyond the antics of the skeptics. Knowledge is held to be certain knowledge. The search for certainty is on. When utter certainty is reached, the foundation of knowledge is revealed. Anything we can then derive from that will also be freed from the threat of doubt. No wonder, then, that rhetoric is cast aside. As philosophy moves toward science, it moves away from rhetoric. That is, it moves away from history, contingency, the inherently perilous and uncertain character of human life, and toward the security of a well-founded epistemology.

Out of this movement comes much of the contents of contemporary philosophy syllabuses. There we will find the representational theory of perception, the incorrigibility of immediate perception, the deliverances of the reason, and much else. The philosophical rhetoric of the anti-rhetorical era moves toward the production of attitudes to inquiry which exclude the figural language of philosophy from serious consideration. There is no possibility that figural thought contributes to our advancing knowledge because it does not connect straightforwardly to the foundations of our knowledge.

This emerges most forcefully in the example I have already discussed, A.J. Ayer's *Language, Truth and Logic*. The foundation of knowledge is the "observation statement." Such statements are merely reports of the immediate sense-contents of the perceptions of an observer. They are paradigmatically "meaningful" and have a definite "sense." What determines the "meaning" of a statement is the possibility of direct observation. For example, "The sky is blue today" is meaningful because we can understand what it is to observe the sky's color. I go outside during the daytime, look up, and if the sky is blue I see that it is. Rather, I see a "blue sense-datum." Every meaningful statement will have links to such basic descriptions of the immediate contents of the observer's perceptions.

Figural language points us to thoughts of things which will never relate back to direct "observation-statements." It thus fails the test of meaningfulness. This is not the time to go into detail about the function of figural language in philosophical writing. The point is that Ayer's foundationalist epistemology works to exclude tropical language from philosophical analysis.

The third era began in the late eighteenth and nineteenth centuries. I have already mentioned Kierkegaard and Nietzsche. They inaugurate a reaction to the dominant philosophical rhetoric of rationalism, empiricism (itself a form of rationalism), and idealism. Instead of working toward a direct expression of what reason tells us, both philosophers take to the use of indirect means to bring about a shift in perceptions and conceptual strategies. However, the attack upon foundationalism and the intellectual stance it requires, comes into its own in the twentieth century. It is with Heidegger, Wittgenstein, and Derrida that this attack comes to a head. I will comment on them very briefly.

With Heidegger the turn comes through the forgotten question of "Being."[12] The dominant categories of western metaphysics obscure "Being" and restrict our reasoning to the "beings" which our already conceptualized world presents to us. This conceptualization, however, is not simply given but is the result of intellectual reflection. There is, argues Heidegger, a "primordial" understanding or orientation of human beings which is prior to any theory about the "foundations" of knowledge. Modern epistemology merely thinks that it begins at the beginning, when, in fact, it begins much further down the line. It is thus mistaken in its initial steps, and it amounts, in the end, to no more than a ramified mistake.

Wittgenstein, too, is critical of attempts to "found" our systems of knowledge. In the *Philosophical Investigations*[13] he distinguishes between foundations and bedrock. We do indeed meet bedrock in our inquiries. But this simply means that we come to the end of the line in our investigations. We can go no further. But what the bedrock is differs in different investigations. Wittgenstein argues that what will count as the point at which our justifications come to an end will depend upon the sort of inquiry we are pursuing. Not all justifications come to an end at the same place.[14] To suppose that all our knowledge claims lead back to a certain and universal "foundation" covers up all those differences that Wittgenstein wishes to reveal.

Derrida, of course, holds that to search for "foundations" in epistemology is to fall prey to the myth of "presence," that somehow we can be in the presence of fundamental truths and thus rest secure. It is to suppose erroneously that we can suspend the operation of *différance* in the case of knowledge and meet the truth face to face. That would be the end of philosophical rhetoric. But it is a myth, a picture, as Wittgenstein would say, which holds us captive. By exploding the myth, Derrida reinserts philosophy into the rhetorical arena.[15]

The three eras outlined here are moments of the dialectic of which I spoke. Philosophy is about both truth and persuasion. The tension which motivates the dialectic comes about because the concepts of truth and persuasion do not sit comfortably together. They have, in Kant's phrase, an "unsocial sociability."[16] They are like star-crossed lovers who find it very difficult to live together, but impossible to live apart. Philosophical rhetoric is their uneasy marriage.

The movement of the dialectic is like that of a pendulum. Now one side of the original opposition between philosophy and rhetoric gains the upper hand, now the other. This is understandable since it is very difficult to forge the language to think the two together as a non-harmonious totality. Part of the problem resides in the differing demands of truth and persuasion. I can be persuaded of a truth, but I can also be persuaded of a falsehood. There is no way within the persuasive context to tell the difference between them. Of course, it is a good idea to argue for the truth of different statements in the course of trying to persuade an audience to believe or do something, but that is not the main issue. The problem is that I can be persuaded that *P*, and *P* is false. My feeling certain or convinced about something does not make it the case.

The distinction between the thought that something is true and its truth independently of that thought is necessary to philosophical inquiry. Without that, philosophy collapses into the rhetoric of the original opposition. Whether we can ever come up with necessary and sufficient conditions for knowledge is a moot point. But we do not have to settle that vexed issue to mark the distinction. If we have no way to appeal to a truth distinguishable from what seems to be true, then talk of truth and knowledge is impossible, and so is the goal of philosophical inquiry, i.e. to arrive at a position which, if true, is so independently of what particular individuals may think about it.

On the view I am putting forward, what we must concede is simply the distinction between the belief that *P* and the truth that *P*. Belief and *P* is one thing, the truth of *P* another. However the issue is decided in any given case, we must grant that the distinction is possible if we wish to proceed in a philosophical investigation. Whether or not we come to a firm conclusion in our investigation, we still have recourse to the questions raised by the possible discrepancy between belief and truth. We need the language of mistake and correction, validity and invalidity, right- and wrong-headedness, etc., in order to continue the work of putting forth and criticizing the different theories and projects which philosophers advance in the course of their work.

This recourse to questioning is like that which emerges from Plato's discussion of justice in the *Republic*. Much the same move is made there in objection to *de dicto* accounts of positive justice. For example, in the discussion which Socrates has with Thrasymachus[17] much of the problem seems to pivot on the fact that they miss each other in speech. They are talking about two different things. Thrasymachus is speaking of justice as it is practiced, Socrates as it ought to be practiced. For Thrasymachus the meaning of "justice" is tied to its application within existing institutions. And in existing institutions justice is the interest of the strongest. Socrates asks if this justice is in fact just.

What Socrates points out and Thrasymachus will not accept or understand, is that it is always possible to ask this question of any law which purports to establish what is just. We can always ask of any law whether it is, itself, just. However, if we ask this question and stick to Thrasymachus' view, there is no way to answer it, since our only appeal is to positive, empirical justice. Socrates is trying to shift the question into a different gear. Thrasymachus will not shift, and that is why their discussion ends in such a desultory fashion.

Socrates is surely in the right here. Even though we may not know what justice is, we may confidently judge that it is not Thrasymachus' "justice." To argue that an act or person is just because his or her actions and character conform to accepted standards of justice is like arguing that a proposition is true simply because one believes it. It is like saying that justice is determined merely by the victors in a struggle for power. There is no distinction between "winner's justice" and justice itself.

Just as we can ask whether a law is just, so we can ask whether the proposition believed is actually true. We should not be pushed into a debate about whether we can actually tell the difference in any given case. This would lead us into all the complexities of the debates which center on the problem of the criterion of truth. My position is not that we can always answer the question in a satisfactory way, but that it is important that we can ask it in the first place. This is part of the regulative use of the principle of truth.

I have argued that it is necessary to philosophical inquiry that we are able to question the truth of a belief. And this truth must be held to transcend the belief structure of individual speakers to be worthy of serious investigation. It must aim in the direction of a truth beyond what is merely taken as true.

If this is indeed a legitimate and necessary aim of philosophical investigation, the temptations of eternity are considerable. Human beings are finite in space and time. Whatever lies outside of space and time transcends the partial and subjective beliefs of individual speakers or writers. In this way we can understand the emphasis on timeless truths in philosophical writing, truths whose objects transcend both time and space, change and contingency. We are introduced to a world of Forms, of timeless truths, eternal necessary being. The aim is to view everything *sub specie aeternitatis* and not *sub specie temporis et loci*. Rhetoric, even philosophical rhetoric, is irredeemably bound to time and situation. It is bound by public institutions and rites, by chance events and the vagaries of public opinion. It is subject to the whims of fashion and the receptivity of its audience. Surely we can leave all that behind in the contemplation of eternal being or the operation of natural laws.

The philosophical rhetoric of the anti-rhetorical moment of the dialectic works the theme of eternity to set itself off from thought bound to the contingencies and practicality of public life. As we saw with Descartes, the reader is invited to go into isolation and ponder the questions of the text, to give up ordinary beliefs and think again from the beginning according to a rational principle. He opens up before us the vista of universal and necessary truth accessible to the reason in each of us. The "I" of the *cogito* is as much a universal principle as a principle of the individual. In reason we meet as one.

Thus the content of anti-rhetorical philosophy reveals its connection with the rhetorical arena in which it is being forged. The dialectical moment of "truth" pushes toward eternity and unchanging realities, toward universality and necessity in its judgments. The drive to speak of a truth which transcends the individual's beliefs makes objective and universal claims more attractive. Eternal truths and the like are the logical limits of an appeal to truth which transcends the conditioned beliefs of individuals, and thus will continue to exert an attraction.

It remains to ask whether the same can be said of the moment of "persuasion" in the dialectic of philosophical rhetoric. The answer is "yes." We can expect that the emphasis on timelessness will be countered by the downplaying of eternity. This is exactly what we find. Using Derrida's terminology, we could say that the cardinal sin of the western tradition in philosophy is its logocentrism. It is important to note that the concepts of "necessity" and "universality," of "atemporality," "substance," and "essence," the principle of reason itself, are all part of the attempted hegemony of reason. They are tied to the "myth of presence" which supports the worship of the *logos* and all it stands for: domination, repression, false clarity, and false closure. It is part of the philosophical rhetoric of the moment of "persuasion" that it downplay the preoccupation with eternal truths and the philosophical stance this implies.

It is precisely what the anti-rhetorical philosophy excludes that is emphasized. Philosophical writing is inscribed in a rhetorical space. It is an intervention in public discourse. All moves which would take us in the direction of a fixed and immutable nature are resisted. All we have is the endless play of signifiers and the exploration of intertextuality. Nothing is ever settled, for the matters arising are always deferred until the next discussion. We never stand in the presence of truth. All we can do is read texts closely and be on the watch for the main thrust of the rhetoric of anti-rhetorical philosophical writings.

What emerges from this brief description is that the case for truth alone and the case for persuasion alone each obliquely involves a reference to the other. They cannot be separated though they can pull in different directions. The case for the rhetoric of the original distinction is impossible apart from its rejection of philosophical truth. It must take its stand with Protagoras[12] and hold that it is human beings who measure the truth, and that truth is that which they so measure.

This view of truth, which makes it relative to the beliefs of the individuals who hold it, locates knowledge not in contemplation of the Forms, but in the ability to shape events. These events are contingent. Our actions have unforeseeable consequences. Yet we must act and the choice is ours. By rejecting a truth which transcends individuals, all our discourse becomes rhetorical in the widest sense.

The ability to "speak well" and move an audience is a sign of knowledge and power. It is a knowledge of how an audience is likely to respond based upon the trial and error of experience. It is a knowledge of such facts as are generally agreed and found acceptable. And finally, it is knowledge of the proper timing and setting in which to speak. The way of rhetoric is based on intuition and ingenuity. It improvises upon the views it shares with the audience or expects the audience to have. It displays agility in meeting unexpected obstacles. The rules of rhetoric include a clause putting the practitioner upon his or her own judgment as to what to say and when to say it. There is really no method to rhetoric, and to this extent Plato is right when he says that rhetoric is not an art (*techne*).[19] He says it is a knack for producing predictable perlocutionary effects in an audience.

We thus have an opposition between philosophy and rhetoric in which each side comes to negate the other while at the same time each finds the other within itself. Philosophy finds itself indissolubly linked to rhetoric, and rhetorical speech finds itself obliged to orientate itself toward the truth. Even if we imagine the most hypocritical of rhetors who argues a case before the assembly and lies through his teeth, he must present his lies as the straightforward truth. While privately denying the existence of a truth beyond what people believe to be true, the rhetor must publicly maintain just this conception of an independent truth. It is no good for the rhetor to admit that his or her beliefs are just as good or as bad as anyone else's. That would be no recommendation for the

91

audience to accept what the rhetor says. What rhetor, if asked whether what he or she said is independently true, would deny it, could afford to deny it? If the answer is "no," then there would be no reason for anyone else to believe it. Someone like Protagoras might teach his relativism to his disciples in private, but publicly he could make no such admission.

There is no formal rhetorical method, but there are rhetorical strategies. Far from discounting truth, rhetorical strategies constantly play upon it, if not in theory, then in practice. A strategy of persuasion must actually court a belief in truth which goes beyond mere opinion. It must come up with a standard of truth by which its own conclusions follow in a manner acceptable to the audience. In this way rhetoric is a slave to truth.

On the other hand, philosophy is also a slave to rhetoric when set in opposition to it. The philosophy/rhetoric distinction is the creation of the philosopher, and turns out to be the philosopher's Frankenstein. For rhetoric is created by the philosopher as a sworn opposition, as enemy and other. This has two main consequences for philosophical writing which attempts to make the distinction.

The first consequence is that the enemy, once created, starts fighting back. We have the battle of philosophy and rhetoric. This means that philosophy must always be on its guard against the machinations of the rhetorical foe. The irony is that the enemy is self-induced and exists only because it has been so posited. A great effort must be made to shore up the weighted dichotomies which run through anti-rhetorical philosophical writing. It is the "return of the repressed." Philosophy attempts to repress its rhetorical nature which then comes back to haunt it in the form of its other. The energy needed to keep rhetoric out of philosophy shows its closeness to that which it excludes. The great images of the Forms, of eternal truths, or reason and the divine mind are all part of rhetorical strategies which have philosophical significance at the same time. Philosophy cannot free itself from rhetoric.

The second consequence is that philosophy must avail itself of rhetorical devices to carry out its repression of rhetoric. We have noted several instances of this. The battle between rhetoric and philosophy is really a battle of differing rhetorics. Thus philosophical writing *contra* rhetoric undermines itself from the outset, since it uses the weapons of the enemy to defeat the enemy. But to do this ensures the victory of rhetoric and so is totally self-defeating.

Both consequences are evidence that the links between philosophy and rhetoric cannot be broken by philosophy since they are forged by philosophy in the very act of making the distinction in the first place. The conclusion is that philosophy and rhetoric are tied to one another, are different but inseparable. The concept of philosophical rhetoric which I am working to develop bridges the gap between philosophy and rhetoric, not by cancelling it, but by recognizing both it and the tensions produced by the different demands of philosophy and rhetoric.

It remains here to ask whether rhetoric and philosophy, persuasion and truth, can pull in the same direction. Certainly Plato thought this possible.[20] There seems to be no logical obstacle. If it is possible to speak or write something true, then it also possible to speak it persuasively or unpersuasively. Whether what is spoken persuasively is true is an issue we do not have to settle now, but it is one which it is legitimate to discuss. We can and do argue about what we can and cannot know, about justifications and reasons for believing this or that. Knowledge is not the issue, but truth and its relation to persuasion. It is clear that if any truth can be expressed in words, its expression will have a rhetorical shape.

This view is compatible with the gamut of epistemological theories. We do not need a "theory" of knowledge to see that truth and persuasion can pull in the same direction despite our ignorance of the truth. Philosophical rhetoric is just the case in which truth and persuasion do pull in the same direction. It is orientated toward promoting the truth which its philosophy seeks or recommends.

This is the case even with those like Nietzsche and Derrida who question the whole concept of truth as handed down in the western philosophical tradition. For Nietzsche the disguised value of truth is the will-to-power; for Derrida, the logocentric position. Yet both try to speak the truth in their own way.

This recognition will not come easily to those philosophers, castigated by Nietzsche and Derrida, who want their truths served up to them in a direct and straightforward manner. There are many approaches to philosophy by which Nietzsche does not look like a philosopher at all, but at best like an inspired madman or poet. We do not find highly structured and systematic arguments, but bald assertions, flashy metaphors, cultivated disdain, *ad hominem* arguments, fits of pique, and outrageous logic. We are told that truth is a dead metaphor which has forgotten itself as metaphor.[21] The philosopher's truth is an illusion. From the standpoint of the opposition Nietzsche is either not a philosopher or is not trying to speak the truth.

If he does not offer a true standpoint from which to understand the world and philosophy in it, he is certainly offering what we are to take to be a superior standpoint or ethos. His "philosophy" is not for everyone, nor can everyone bear its "truth" (that there is no truth). But otherwise Nietzsche's superior standpoint bears all the marks of truth. That is, Nietzsche is not speaking to himself alone. He addresses a small audience, and tries to make the reader feel part of that exclusive group of superior minds. He uses indirect means to wean the reader from the traditional concept of truth, but he also leaves the reader with the truth so few wish to grasp. For if Nietzsche is right, then it is true that "truth" is nothing but a human projection. Furthermore, this "truth" is not true because Nietzsche enunciates it, but he enunciates it because he judges it to be true. (Think of the tone of Nietzsche's philosophical rhetoric: self-confident and self-righteous.)

If this were not so, it is hard to see why Nietzsche spends so much time undermining the philosophical tradition in which he finds himself. He castigates philosophers repeatedly for their mistakes and self-deceptions, and yet also seems to reserve room for a philosophy of which he is the philosopher. Nietzsche is a philosopher against philosophers. He exposes their philosophical rhetoric, the perlocutionary actions and effects which act as ulterior motives, if you will, of philosophical discourse and writing. He threatens philosophical theories with their own rhetoric and seems to reduce philosophy to it.

However, we do not have to interpret Nietzsche in this way. Once we detach the dialectic of truth and persuasion from the question of epistemology, we can begin to see the shape of Nietzsche's rhetorical philosophy. His attacks on foundational epistemologies of whatever stripe have no direct bearing upon the question of whether Nietzsche's philosophy claims a truth for itself which transcends his own rhetorical statement of it. Nietzsche argues his truth, which is not his alone, but exists for all rare spirits who can join him on the mountain peaks. It is not a truth which can be expressed directly in the dry and static prose of the philosophers. It cannot be expressed directly at all.

Nietzsche takes the path of indirection to argue his truth. But neither his truth nor his argument fits comfortably within a philosophy which eschews rhetoric. Everyone will surely agree that if Nietzsche is a philosopher at all, he is a highly rhetorical one. He does not play by the rules of academic philosophy. But he does have an argument of a sort, a perlocutionary argument. He strategically employs a concatenation of devices and tactics to persuade his small audience to break with the delusions and myths to which they have been subject and say "no." Just say "no" to metaphysics. Say "yes" to imagination.

There is, in the end, no set of self-consistent Nietzschean propositions. There is no one "philosophy" of Nietzsche which can take its place on the roster of "philosophies." A perlocutionary argument does not have a proposition as its conclusion but an effect in the way the audience looks and feels about things, a change in philosophical ethos.

Because Nietzsche is trying to break with the dominant tradition of philosophical authority, and since that authority expresses the sentiments of an anti-rhetorical era, it is not surprising that his writing is full of "literary" devices, poetic indirection, persuasion, and the rest. For example, his writing may shock us, and coming to be shocked is a perlocutionary effect of what he writes. These effects are due not only to the content of what he says but also to the context. His writing may produce many such effects which together move the reader in unexpected directions. They are part of a philosophical rhetoric which makes full use of the means of indirect communication, much of which comes from the rhetorical tradition. As we have seen, not all philosophical stances have made such full use of them.

We find the same sort of result in the writing of Derrida. The enunciation of *différance*, the demolition of logocentrism as a last word, the convoluted and difficult language, all point to a rhetorician's philosopher. Both Nietzsche and Derrida turn to rhetorical language to find the resources to combat the falsifications and mystifications surrounding and informing the dominant culture and its means of expression.

The trouble is that the dominant modes of expression in a culture cannot be directly supplanted and erased, because direct expression is retained for the dominant modes themselves. Thus it would be impossible to make Nietzschean or Derridean points in the language of logocentrism, let alone make them convincingly. Neither antagonist argues directly with the opponent, for to engage in a contest in the first place is already to concede it. What can be done to make room for an alternative? Mobilize the resources of indirect communication. Find a different language. This different language is precisely the one excluded from anti-rhetorical philosophy, the language of rhetoric itself.

Nietzsche and Derrida are highly rhetorical philosophers in the conventional sense of the word. Their writing is full of word-play, metaphor, paradox, and the rejection of that "clarity" and "distinctness" which have characterized much philosophical writing. But they are still philosophers for all that, for their rhetoric serves the truth, even if the truth cannot be known. They are both attempting, through perlocutionary arguments, to effect a change in the outlook of the audience through which their truth will out.

In Derrida's case we must break out of slavish obedience to a law which is not our own, and yet we can never completely sever our links with it. The logocentric position, to be sure, is deconstructed. Its oppositions and valuations are laid bare. Its rhetoric is exposed. But without the logocentric position there would be nothing to deconstruct. We will continue to argue about the truth of different matters, while at the same time we can learn to deconstruct the discourse of truth. And this is the truth: we can do both.

I will conclude this chapter by way of summary and stage setting for what is to follow. The main point is that, rightly understood, philosophical discourse and writing aim at truth. This truth must be conceived to stand independently of its enunciation or its enunciator. At the same time truth is enunciated in a rhetorical arena. One can try to exclude philosophy from rhetoric and perhaps rhetoric from philosophy, but neither strategy will work. Instead, we must grasp the concept of a philosophical rhetoric which takes an independent truth as its goal and uses indirection as the means to bring about a perspective in the audience from which that truth can be seen.

Indirect communication involves the attempt to bring about changes in the audience. In the case of philosophical rhetoric these changes will relate to the appreciation of a truth; not one, however, that can be directly expressed in propositions. This indirection is part of philosophical writing in general. Within it there are poles.

Roughly speaking, one sort is pro-rhetoric and one is anti-rhetoric. As poles, we never find pure examples. There is rhetoric in the writings of the most severely anti-rhetorical philosophers, and there are direct and straightforward arguments in the most elusive of the pro-rhetorical philosophers.

I have been working toward a dialectical conception of philosophical rhetoric which allows us to assimilate the contributions of persuasion and truth to philosophical discourse, without forcing us to abandon one or the other as an irrelevancy or falsehood. Philosophers stand to gain in self-consciousness by assimilating the role of rhetoric in their practice of philosophy. It is not embarrassing or shameful to ask philosophical questions, to aim for a truth that transcends the individual through a rational dialogue. Philosophy should recover its nerve without closing its mind.

The anti-rhetorical phase of philosophical investigation seems to have crested. There is an opportunity now to investigate the rhetorical side of philosophy without prejudice to the inquiry itself. It is in this spirit that I will pass on to a consideration of rhetorical tropes in philosophical writing. It will emerge that it is through the use of tropes, and especially metaphors, that philosophical writing produces much of the indirect impact it requires to have an effect upon an audience and its conception or feeling for truth.

Chapter Four

TROPICAL PHILOSOPHY

The task of this chapter is to examine the use of figural language in philosophical texts. Normally when we are asked questions about figures of speech and style it is in connection with poetry and fiction. It is in poetry, *par excellence*, that we find full use of metaphor, metonymy, synecdoche, irony, and the other poetic tropes. The appeal of poetry seems to exceed that of philosophy. While philosophy addresses our minds, poetry addresses our hearts. It stirs up passions and emotions. It creates moods. It leads us not only to think but also to feel.

There is a close connection, if not an outright identity, between poetry and rhetoric. Poetry is the extreme example of a writing which is many-layered and highly complex. The effects it produces in readers are also complex and touch them in different ways. If rhetoric and poetry are different, it is in their ends rather than their means. Traditional rhetorical activity takes place in a public arena where action is to be decided. Poetic activity is also carried out in a public arena, but for the most part there is no particular action or choice which results from it.

Poetic writing lies outside the orbit of purely instrumental communication. Traditionally, poetry is the teacher of humankind. Its voice instructs the people. Ancient poetic instruction takes place in a space opened up by the severing of instrumental links to the immediate environment. Though it might be that the information contained in poetry is acted upon out of pragmatic interest, the learning of it is a moment apart from the ordinary pursuits of life. In an oral community this means listening to the words of the bard and concentrating on them. Perhaps it is possible to listen to the bard and do one's knitting, but more demanding work must cease.

The point of this short excursion into a priori anthropology is to render plausible the view that in the rhythm of daily life in pre-literate cultures, poetic recitation had a special place. The use of poetic conventions set its speech off from the ordinary instrumental communication of the people. To listen to poetic language and recognize it as such is already to set it outside the ordinary contexts of communication. The language of poetry is an exalted one, suitable for expressing the highest dreams and deepest fears of the people. Poetry has the power to create an imaginary world and mold collective life.

The subjects of Greek myth are larger than life. We are introduced to a symbolic world of signs and meanings beyond the compass of ordinary life. The audience is lifted out of itself and sees itself reflected and magnified through its poetry. Poetic language opens up a gap in the world of daily life which makes the creation of other worlds possible. Using the language of phenomenology we can say that poetry invites the transcendence of the audience, offers a loss of self which is an enlargement of self.

The Greek word *poesis* connotes an activity of making or creating something. The ancient poet is a maker, someone who creates a world of imagination out of nothing. The poems touch and move individuals as a group, give them a collective identity and provide a framework of ideas within which it is possible to think about the world together and respond to it.

The audience which listens to the poets will begin to feel as one, the individuals lost in an experience which transcends them all. The Greeks become Greeks through an exercise of imagination. Their poets invent the Greek mind. Their philosophers sift and refine the poetic materials and leave us with the idea of a "critique" of poetry and poetic constructions.

Philosophy is tied to poetry much in the way it is tied to rhetoric. The poetic resources of language are also the resources of philosophical indirection. And since philosophical writing is never entirely free of indirect or perlocutionary effects, we should avail ourselves of poetry to help us to understand the indirections of philosophical writing. We should ask about the role of poetic tropes in philosophical discourse and be on the look-out for them in the literature. What emerges will illuminate the nature of philosophical rhetoric.

To begin, let us reflect once again upon the old dispute between philosophy and poetry. There is no doubt that poetry and rhetoric, in the sense of persuasive and elegant speech, are both far older than philosophy. From the point of view of poetry, philosophy is a young upstart who belittles its elders and betters with reckless disregard for the consequences, and the consequences are dire.

I will not go through the entire litany of grievances which poetry can invoke but there are a few which deserve to be called to our attention. Philosophy awakens a questioning spirit in the people who become infected with it. They cannot stop asking questions. Furthermore, they cannot stop criticizing what they hear or read. Always carping, always nit-picking, the philosopher is fastidious in logic and honor-bound to point out mistakes in the reasoning of others.

The philosophers use their newly forged *logos* as a stick to beat *poesis* from the field. This is not fair or right, and is dangerous. The imaginative constructions of a collectively held poetry actually create the peoples of the world by bringing into being what Vico calls the *sensus communis* of the people.[1] Philosophy, by positing the supremacy of an abstract universality, separates the people. Philosophy sets people off from one another by having them think for themselves, ask questions, criticize traditional wisdom and always seek the "rational" argument.

Of course poetry, like rhetoric, is not designed to answer philosophical questions and hence fails to do a very good job at answering them. But as in the case of rhetoric, the dispute between poetry and philosophy is started by philosophy. To define itself, philosophy produces its others: rhetoric is one, poetry another. Let us look at the matter from the perspective of an anti-poetic philosophy.

A good starting place is Plato's celebrated critique of poetry.[2] According to Plato's narrative there are a number of things wrong with poetry. Poetry, like rhetoric, appeals to our emotions, not to our reason. The poets are indeed inspired, but that is a drawback. Some of their utterances may be divine, but what this means is that the poet does not understand what he or she is saying. The poets are incapable of supplying the *logos* of their creations or productions. (Drama counts as poetry.) They cannot say what they mean in straightforward discursive prose. This has the unfortunate effect of making it very difficult, if not impossible, to tell which of the poet's utterances accord with truth and which are fraudulent.

If the poets cannot give the *logos* or account of what they are saying, what is the status of the interpreters of poetry? Are they any better off? The answer would seem to be "no," for it is as difficult to tell which interpretation of a poem is the "correct" one as it is to tell which bits of poetry are "true." The critics put forward competing *logoi* (readings) and differing interpretations. They do not agree about how to determine which *logos* or interpretation is to be preferred. Disputes are interminable. The form and content of poetic writing have no clearly defined boundaries. It is impossible to say what the final reading or interpretation of a poem will look like. There is only the next reading. Critics are in the same position as the poets themselves. Neither possesses a *logos* which can be expressed in straightforward prose.

From the perspective of embattled philosophy, however, it is not possible to examine poetry closely without ambivalence. The world of poetry strikes the anti-poetic philosopher as a maddeningly indeterminate field of meaning in which nothing can be put to rest or settled. At the same time that is its undoubted power. Poetry has effects upon its audience which surpass any interpretation which can be affixed to particular poems. Its power is to effect an imaginative break with the world as an instrumental context. This power is also a danger. Doubts arise about the uses to which this power is put. Plato is clear both in his admiration for the poet's genius and in his awareness of the dangers of allowing unregulated poetic production. Not all "good" poetry is good, not all of it is true. It is the job of philosophy to recognize what is good and true in a poem and what is not. The false and bad poetry must be eliminated, and all poetry must be regulated by a higher philosophical conception of the Good. Poetry must be made fit for admission to Plato's republic.

If we listen to Plato's story, poetry is a scandal. Homer, the most divine of poets, has the gods and goddesses do the most immoral things. Zeus often changes shape and seduces or rapes earth women just out of lust. All of the gods are guilty of meddling in human affairs for their own amusement. They are portrayed as acting unjustly, cheating, lying, stealing, and so forth. Their characters are hardly without blemish. Taken all in all, Homer's Olympians are an unsavory bunch. They may be immortal, beautiful, and stronger than we are, but they are not paragons of moral virtue (*arete*).

Plato suggests that we remove the offensive passages from Homer, leaving only those which pass the censorship of philosophy. Philosophy and the philosopher king sit in judgment upon poets and poetry. This is as it should be. The end or *telos* of human life is moral excellence. Everything which conduces to this end is admirable and praiseworthy. Everything which thwarts it is base and shameful. Poetry cultivates a language of feeling and memory. The feelings are called up by the remembered words, and the best poetry is full of memorable images and vivid sayings. Like oatmeal, poetry sticks to the ribs. If it moves an audience toward moral excellence, well and good. If not, then that poetry is not suited to the end and must be rejected.

The problem is that poetry is not self-regulating. It lacks moderation and temperance (*sophrosune*). Poetry and poetic genius are akin to madness. Plato thinks that we see this quite plainly in the theater. There, actors speaking poetry move large audiences to the brink of madness themselves. What horror is not wrought upon the stage of Greek tragedy? The audience is witness to unspeakable events through the words of the poet. The tragedy is designed to touch our deepest fears and nightmares and give them collective expression. Whether or not the tragedy is completed by catharsis, as Aristotle claims, it evokes strong emotions in the audience, impeding rational thought.

Drama is singled out for particular criticism by Plato,[3] in part because it produces a collective hysteria. In a crowd individuals no longer behave as they do when alone. They are "swept away" in a current of emotion produced by the crowd as a whole. *Logos* is swamped by *pathos*. This is one of the reasons Socrates prefers to speak with individuals rather than to groups.

Furthermore, the way tragic *pathos* is produced leaves something to be desired. There is no control or reason in it. The playwright writes his tragedy in part to hear the acclaim of the crowd and win the competition. This is the goal of Greek immortality, to find a place in the memory of the people. However, it is a goal which is extraneous to the end of moral excellence. The poet must please the audience. This is not the most noble of motives. There is always the temptation to play upon the audience and manipulate it in various ways. The poets of the stage invite us to experience emotions vicariously which we would never allow ourselves to feel outside the theater. The tragic poets ask us to contemplate and feel the horrors of human existence; comic poets ask us to laugh at them. Either way we are dealing with matters that are shameful and not fitting the character of a "true" human being. Such a person resists the temptation to "lose control" or to be open to irrational persuasion and absurd imaginings. The theater blatantly provides just such temptation.

The connection with rhetoric is clear. The rhetor also aims to sway large gatherings of people, to create an atmosphere in which his or her plans will be furthered. Anyone who has witnessed the films of Hitler's speeches at the giant Nazi rallies of the 1930's cannot fail to be impressed by the impassioned response his speeches provoked. There is something fearful about hundreds of thousands of people mindlessly shouting the same slogans over and over. This is exactly the sort of thing which Plato finds offensive in the power of rhetoric to move people.

Hitler's speech-making had dire political consequences. Perhaps poetry has dire psychological consequences. The poet's audience is encouraged to feel and think in ways which exceed the bounds of propriety. It is very possible that by thinking and feeling the wrong things our moral character is slowly and unconsciously moved in a negative direction. Plato thought it might make us too "womanly"; that is, prone to emotional excesses. Too much poetry may lose us our civic courage and make us effeminate. Too much of the wrong sort of poetry might have the effect of creating a world of fantasy in which to live. We might become dreamers if we listen to the poets, and our lives become a dream. We might miss our chance to emerge from the fantasy world of poetry to the truth of philosophy.

I will not rehearse all the grievances which philosophy can list against poetry. The interesting point is that Plato uses his critique of poetry and the poets to highlight the desirability of philosophy. This is his philosophical rhetoric at work. Where the inspired poet, without knowing what he is doing, produces his works in ignorance, the philosopher makes self-consciousness and self-knowledge his goal. Poetry appeals to the heart, philosophy to the head. Poetry uses indirect techniques to create a climate of feeling regardless of its moral content. Philosophy eschews such techniques in favor of purely rational ones. Poetry must please, philosophy instruct. Poetry deals in illusions, philosophy in truth.

If Plato can but hook the reader on his truth, poetry goes by the wayside. A set of values follows in the wake of the reader's acceptance of Plato's position. The reader's judgment is led in certain directions. For example, we will find the emphasis on universality and necessity which has already been pointed out. Positive value is placed on order, control, harmony, reason, and knowledge. Poetry displays the opposites of these: disorder, lack of control, dissonance, irrationality, and ignorance.

Truth and poetry play off each other. In Plato's philosophical rhetoric they invite a movement of thought which leads from the desire of pleasure and seeming wisdom to truth. This is the job of all the unflattering descriptions of poetry. They gain their point in the contrast they provide to the flattering descriptions of philosophy. To all those who have listened to Plato's call for moral excellence and have cultivated a desire for virtue, negative descriptions of poetry will seem "natural," convincing, and a basis for censorship.

For the reader who is not persuaded to desire moral excellence as Plato outlines it, the weight of these arguments against poetry diminish considerably. Plato's rhetoric is philosophical in so far as its direction is toward philosophical reflection and recollection. It is rhetoric, none the less. For those who are not convinced that the basic question of human existence is "What is the best way for a human to live?", the attempt to answer it will not be as pressing as Plato claims.

Plato's Socrates continually reiterates the principle that caring for the soul is the single most important thing we can do with our lives. The reader who finds Socrates convincing on this point will more readily follow him in a renunciation of poetry than one who is not. Love of Beauty will take us to the Good. Art, as imitation, is but a pale and distorted vision of Beauty itself. Proper care of the soul consists in a proper education of the soul in excellence. We see this most clearly in Plato's elaborate course of education for the philosopher king outlined in the *Republic*.[4]

There are a number of salient features in these sections of the *Republic* for our assessment of poetry. One is the concern which Plato shows for the young.[5] Poetry, as that which is spoken, enters most easily into young minds. If it is repeated endlessly, the child soon has a large stock of poetic conceits and poem fragments populating his or her imagination. These form the basis of a world of fantasy which may have little or nothing to do with the world of truth Plato would have us attain. Nevertheless, they are there.

They take root and grow ambiguous layers of meaning. Poems give a multitude of "sayings," sanctioned by convention, which can be uttered and taken in with little or no conscious thought or effort. I count as poetry all the maxims, fables, old wives' sayings, political advertizing slogans, catch-phrases, and poetic verses which have passed over into the public domain; the common coin of non-philosophical conversation.

Another point allied to the first is that poetry, for much of its existence, was designed to be memorized and memorizable. This is important because a poem only exists in words and in the memory of words. We can possess a poem as we possess nothing else in this life. It is a constant resource for thinking or feeling about the world and our life within it. If I have memorized a poem it is mine because with the words I have the whole poem. There is nothing left out. To memorize a poem is to take away that which it is in itself. There is no difference between what a poem is in itself and what it is for us. There is no difference between appearance and reality. So it is a real possession.[6]

Memorizing a poem, however, does not guarantee that it is understood or thought about to any significant extent. It is very possible to memorize a poem and not have the vaguest idea what it means. One can know a poem without understanding it. However, the reverse does not hold. It is impossible to understand a poem without knowing it. This does not mean that a poem must be memorized to be understood, but that at least one must have reference to a familiar text. Memorizing a poem simply severs the links to any particular copy of the text.

From a Platonic perspective this makes poetry a very great potential danger. If the wrong poem worms itself into the mind of a susceptible individual, it may spread its poison through the entire character. A poem sticks to the mind like glue, so we must be very careful which poems we are to allow entry to the mind. For Plato, admissible poems are those which praise a purified divinity and the heroes of the *polis*.[7] If a particular poem is bad, then the complete possession of it through memory is even worse. The possession of a bit of poetry gives it time to work its magic on the soul, with results which cannot be known before it sets to work. Hence it is the job of a wise censor to pick and choose suitable poems for impressionable minds incapable of judging the future effects of incorporating them into their mental economy.

Unreflective acceptance of poetic sayings has an impact on how we think and feel, the effects of which are unconscious in the individual. A poem is like a narcotic; it stupefies the mind while at the same time stirring up images, feelings, and emotions. Its indirect effects are brought about surreptitiously, behind the mental backs of the audience.

Plato himself is clear about this. In the *Theaetetus* he puts the poet above the rhetorician precisely because of the indirection and hence discretion of the poet.[8] The poet speaks with many voices but only to those who can hear. The rhetorician brings the mystery out of hiding and displays it for all to see, whether the audience is capable of understanding it or not.

The case at issue in the *Theaetetus* concerns the claim of Protagoras that human being is the measure of all things, both of what is and what is not. Poets had already implied the same conclusion, but not on the basis of an explicit argument to that effect. The terrible truth of relativism can be discerned in the writings of the poets, but only for those who are prepared. The poems can be read in ways which slide around the terrible truth. Like the duck-rabbit, you either see the duck or you do not (see p. 75). The poem can be interpreted as hinting at the dark truth, but it never comes right out and says it. Therefore, the sophists and rhetoricians are worse than the poets who at least have the courtesy to hide their meaning through indirection.

Philosophy creates itself through the creation of its others. Rhetoric and poetry are two. Why, in particular, those two? I have already suggested an answer in terms of the extra-rational appeals which poetry and rhetoric make upon their audiences. We are in a position now to grasp another reason. Let us consider poetry first and then come back to rhetoric.

Poetry, we recall, has the facility to slip unnoticed into the mind, there to work its good or ill. Poetry also has a very close connection with memory and has its very existence in words. Remembering the words of a poem and recalling them on different occasions slowly give them meaning and significance. The poem reveals to us more and more of its hidden meanings. We can see deeper and deeper into it. We have more and more to say about it if we reflect on it. This is one way it can go.

Another way a poem can go is simply to become part of a stock repertoire of pre-digested thoughts and images, unthinkingly grasped and employed; poetic fragments used in place of thought. Remembered poetry can induce a kind of forgetfulness in the person who incorporates it into his or her repertoire. It can become a kind of shield for use against thought in the name of a spurious wisdom.

Poets can acquire an unwarranted authority. The mere fact that a poem or poetic fragment is mentally at hand to be recited does not mean that it is well thought out. It may simply be convenient. Yet the poem exists and speaks in the voice of authority. To take it in unreflectively is to absorb this voice as authoritative, but without considering its basis. In the *Ion* Socrates has great fun with the young rhapsode who quotes Homer as *the* authority upon every matter of which he speaks.[9] Needless to say under Socratic cross-questioning Ion is unable to defend either himself or Homer from the inconsistencies and errors thus exposed. It is too easy simply to quote the great poet and to consider that that absolves one from the task of further thought. Poetic memory can be a form of amnesia.

Having said this, it is important to recognize that not all uses of poetic memory are in contradiction with Platonic recollection. There are similarities which make Plato uneasy and defensive when confronted by the ambiguous face of poetry. The parallels are worth exploration.

The story of Platonic recollection is embedded in a myth. At a time before birth the soul of a human being sees directly the eternal reality of all things. In the *Phaedrus* we are told that the souls, trailing behind their respective deities, whirl along the outer edge of heaven gazing at the Beings beyond.[10] In the *Republic* we are told that to be born each of us must drink from the waters of *lethe*[11] through which we enter the world forgetful of the eternal Forms. (Even the gods whirl through the vault of heaven looking out at Beings beyond themselves.)

We have fallen into our bodies and they act as sinkers to pull us down into the depths of the earth rather than draw us to heaven and the Beings beyond. Our job now is to try and catch a glimpse, however indirectly, of those Beings which we once knew (*gignosko*) but have now forgotten. Recollection is the means by which the soul comes to re-establish some connection to those Beings from which it has been severed by birth. Unfortunately for us, our bodies tend to pull us down from our highest aspirations. Our vision is obscured. The result is that in this embodied life we will never entirely recapture that vision which is free of the encumbrances of the body.

The best we can do is to purify ourselves of preoccupation with the body and its desires through dialectic and philosophical recollection. We must cultivate that form of memory which brings self-knowledge and at least an indirect acquaintance with the Forms of things. Our powers of recollection should aim at objects outside our immediate experience, not at those in the changing world of words and finite objects. We should look toward a transcendent world of Forms, not to their imitations in poetry. Perhaps over the course of many lives we may escape altogether from the shadow world of birth and death and attain for eternity that vision of a transcendent reality the soul once had.

Plato resorts to myth at crucial points in his arguments. He uses poetic discourse when rational prose loses its grip, when what is required is not so much intellectual competence as a vision or image projected in the imagination. It is clear in the *Phaedrus*, for example, that Socrates will not stand for rationalistic or reductionist interpretations of myths.[12] Myths, therefore, have something to tell us about ourselves which cannot be explained away through the mechanical application of rational analytic techniques.

Plato has Socrates tell mythical stories when direct and straightforward prose fails him. I say that straightforward prose language fails him, not that his narration of myth is a failure. The knowledge sought cannot be expressed directly in words. As Plato acknowledges in the *Republic*, the ultimate vision of the Good cannot be produced automatically by the educational process.[13] For Plato "higher education" consists in training in dialectic. We learn there to listen and speak, to ask and answer questions, to reflect and analyze, but we cannot be taught to recollect the Forms. The knowledge we seek is within each of us, but we have forgotten it. Therefore, we must look within ourselves for the truth and will look in vain for it in the authority of the philosophers. No book can contain it, no text express it directly. Plato has Socrates point in the direction he is looking. The audience is invited to look in the same direction. However, the looking is a perlocutionary effect of the text's indirection and not within the direct control of the author or his main character, Socrates.

The perlocutionary effects of philosophical writing are the result of the intended or unintended application of indirect means of communication. These means are importantly those of poetic expression. In poetry the audience is invited to enter a world of the imagination where the weight of practical necessity is temporarily lifted. He or she is invited to make sense of the poem, dared to find some meaning in it. As in the case of rhetoric, poetry is tied to its audience in the effects it can produce in them. The poet, and I am speaking here more of the ancient poet than the modern, relies upon the common assumptions, aspirations, fears, and desires of the audience for his or her effects upon them. When times and assumptions have changed, the effects which can be produced through indirection in poetry will also change. It is very likely that the perlocutionary effects now produced by Plato's writing are very different from those it produced in its first audience.

Consider the perlocutionary effects Plato's writing might produce in a feminist audience. Plato is the closest example of a feminist that the ancient world can boast of. In the *Republic*[14] women attain near parity with men. His all-male audience would have gone into shock had he proceeded any further. Nevertheless, when we read that poetry will make us soft and effeminate, it is hard not to notice a philosophical rhetoric that promotes a sexual division between human beings and produces a pernicious nest of oppositions in which women and female traits are associated with the body, while the male ones are associated with mind and the achievement of *nous* and *dianoia*.

If we look at Plato from the perspective of a modern feminist, it is easy to see that some of the perlocutionary effects of his writing might very well be anger and annoyance. This is not a perlocutionary effect which Plato planned to produce. It is nevertheless one which can take effect on the basis of Plato's own philosophical rhetoric. The opposition male/female is in parallel with the others we have examined thus far. It stands in the battery of oppositions which invite philosophical investigation and recollection, and downplay everything which pertains to history and the changing conditions of life under the moon.

It is not surprising, therefore, that Plato turns to the narrative of myths at crucial points in his arguments. There are points at which no rational argument can have the desired effect. At best such an argument can produce an intellectual conviction. Plato wants more than this. He wants nothing less than that the reader or audience change his or her whole way of life, thought, and feeling. By his writing Plato aims to effect a radical change in his audience, to produce a number of perlocutionary effects. The use of myth is one way to accomplish this end and produce the desired effects. Not that it must. A myth can backfire. It is open to varying interpretations. The audience or reader once again plays a crucial role in making sense of a myth. Plato points. It is up to the audience to follow his direction, signposted by the main channel of his philosophical rhetoric.

To speak of the many layers of mythical narrative is to indicate the many different responses which a myth can occasion. Myths have a double nature. We may speak of a surface rendering of myth in contrast to a depth rendering. Plato is acting the poet in the narration of myth. There is one story on the surface of the myth but another story underneath. We who read the story can take it either way. The myth will accommodate us in any case. The ambiguous status of myth as a vehicle of interpretation guarantees that it has the widest range of appeal. It will accommodate audiences coming at it with different skills and experiences, who pick up the thread at different points, and who carry on at their own pace. Reading Plato is very like going through a computer-assisted course of self-teaching in which one proceeds from the level one has already attained to higher levels at the pace most suited to one's own abilities and inclinations.

Plato uses myths to say what cannot be said in straightforward explicit prose. It is not illocutionary success which is required, but perlocutionary success. Myths, as it were, are among the premises of perlocutionary arguments which "go through" if the appropriate perlocutionary effects come about. In Plato's case these are the ones which lead to a "turning of the soul" away from this world to another better one.[15] Plato's myths paint vivid and memorable pictures of both worlds, pictures which stay with the mind and reveal what is at stake in his arguments.

Wittgenstein has argued extensively that the problem with philosophy as traditionally conceived is that the mind is captured by a picture. Our intelligence is bewitched by the philosophical language that we speak.[16] If uncritically accepted, Platonic myths have all the drawbacks which Plato discovers in poetry. The myths themselves are poems. There is a danger that audiences will simply allow themselves to be taken in by the pictures and think no further on the matter. A myth can quickly become dogma unless a critical spirit invests its reception.

How better to do that than to undermine poetic language? This is exactly what Plato does. He may suffer from essentialism, as Wittgenstein alleges, but his mythical pictures are not to take possession of our reason. They are reminders assembled for a particular purpose.[17] The goal is recollection of the Forms which lie beyond mythical representation. Yet paradoxically Plato uses myth itself to put forward images in which it is tempting to lose oneself.

The problem is that poetry seems to foster bad and forgetful memories, not recollection of the Forms. It is true that we have access to the in-itself of a poem once we have memorized it. We can call it up to muse upon or use it in our speech and writing. We do not have to think about it very much. This bad memory of poetry fosters the illusion that the words of the poets have an invulnerability which mortal words do not. This is a mistake. Poetry must answer philosophy.

Consider proper recollection. The things of this world are reminders of another world of which we can have no direct perception here. Yet our minds can be drawn to them through the catalyst of the things in this world which resemble them. From seeing the world through the eyes of the body we can move to seeing it through the eyes of the mind. From particulars we are reminded of the universals in which they participate. This is the familiar Platonic story.

Platonic recollection is this movement from the world of changing particulars to the world of unchanging and timeless Forms. How can we grasp such things unless we have been previously acquainted with them? Whatever works toward re-awakening the sense of acquaintance with the Forms is recollection in the proper sense. Poetry, though it does encourage memory, gives the false impression that poetic language is authoritative without further investigation. We will think alike, but whether we will also think truly is another matter.

I agree with Plato that poetry may encourage non-philosophical habits of thought and that poems can be assimilated unknowingly. Nevertheless, this is only one way in which poetic memory can be used. Another way, which I adverted to above, has to do with a slowly dawning comprehension or understanding of a poem which comes with time and repeated reflection. In many ways it turns out that poetic memory in this sort of case has significant similarities to Platonic recollection.

To begin with, the Forms are eternal entities beyond change and chance. They exist in themselves and by themselves and have no need of anything else in order to be. We are unable to gaze on these Forms directly for our senses will not bear it. Only when we shut out the world and isolate the mind can we "see" what is as it is. The Forms are thus necessary and universal.

On the face of it, Forms and poetry are very different. Poems come into being in time. They are spoken aloud or written down. Other people listen to or read them. We can speak of the vicissitudes of a poem, its ups and downs of repute and value, its loss or discovery, and so on. In that sense a poem is anything but an eternal and universal object. Nevertheless, the words of a poem make up the being of the poem and so are the poem. One can know a poem as few other things in this world. Understanding it is another matter, and one which requires something very like Platonic recollection.

One memorizes a poem. This is like gazing on the Form. One forgets the poem when one is neither actively either memorizing or rehearsing it. The poem has become a possession of the bearer. After the poem is thoroughly memorized it comes to mind from time to time, nominated by some happening in the world. One remembers the poem, has it before one's mind. But it is no longer the same poem. It is not the words of the poem that have changed but one's understanding of those words as seen from a different standpoint. It takes time and recollection to understand a poem properly, and to do that is not totally unlike coming to understand the Forms.

Plato's Forms are conceived to lie beyond dependency upon anything outside themselves. Poems do depend upon poets for their production and hence are not like the Forms. They do, however, have the kind of necessity and completeness which we recognize in the Forms. Though a poem comes into being through the work of the poet, once it has been produced it becomes finished and attains its *telos* (completeness).[18] The finished poem has a kind of necessity which we do not find in the contingent historical world. We know that Achilles will sulk in his tent. We know that Odysseus will escape the Sirens. From the time that the *Iliad* was written down, the tale comes out the same way every time. All the events recur upon each reading and, from the second reading on, the reader already knows how the poem will go. This is part of the great charm of poetry: that it is so reliable. If I want a good tragedy, all I have to do is pick up *Oedipus Rex* and read again the fate of that great king. I would not be able to do this if sometimes when I picked it up, I found it transformed into a comedy.

A poem is as unchanging as the Forms, but our understanding of it does change. The effort required to understand a poem is like that required to recollect the Forms. It is not exhausted in a moment but grows through a lifetime of education, reflection, and experience. The Forms never change, but we do. And each of us must recollect them through our own efforts. There are no short cuts to the Forms. When Plato has Socrates speak of the turning of the soul, he has in mind the point at which the individual is freed from the imperatives of the body and can begin to reflect on the cosmos and the place of the individual within it. This is not a sudden illumination but a slowly growing one, like the understanding of a poem which comes with time and experience.

We cannot arrive at the Forms by the route of direct philosophical argument. The flaws and paradoxes in the theory of the Forms are notorious. Plato himself is aware of the problems with the theory. In the *Parmenides*[19] Plato has Socrates suffer embarrassment at the hands of his venerable interlocutor. He is made to acknowledge his ignorance of the very objects his theory promotes.

At times this has been seen as an outright refutation of the theory of Forms; and as a theory, perhaps, the criticism is well placed. However, if we take Plato's philosophical rhetoric seriously, then the flaws in the theory no more refute it than the flaws of mythical narration refute myth. The "theory of the Forms," rightly understood, is much more like a myth than a theory. Understanding the Forms is more like the appropriation of the meaning of a poem than the analysis of a theoretical system. On their own, both poetic and philosophical language break down. What holds them together is the dialectical tension generated between them. The genius of Plato is that he is capable of bringing home this insight indirectly by displaying the self-subversion of philosophy and poetry. Hence, Plato resorts extensively to myths and poetic devices in the working out of his philosophical rhetoric. We are to reiterate the texts, reflect on them, and slowly an inner meaning will emerge. Once we have seen this inner meaning, then the flaws in Plato's rational argument will matter as little to us as they did to him. Knowing our ignorance, we must begin with poetry to end beyond it, and that beyond is never present to us so long as we remain embodied.

We are to witness the hubris of direct philosophical argument which pretends to truth. We are also to witness the hubris of poetic discourse which pretends to authority. Philosophy and poetry feed off each other and also negate each other. We feel this tension in the paradox that Plato uses poetic techniques to deny that poetry is adequate to the truth. It is the same with rhetoric and philosophical argument. Each is part of Plato's philosophical rhetoric, and each indirectly refutes itself when taken in isolation.

Plato is an anti-poetic poet, an anti-rhetorical rhetorician, and finally an anti-philosophical philosopher. It is true that Plato has Socrates practice rational analysis whenever possible. High words of praise are heaped on the concept of *logos*. We are to work on a rational principle of description and explanation and must not accept a belief or theory which cannot present an adequate account of itself. We know the stringent conditions which Plato has Socrates place upon adequate belief. We do not find many adequate accounts of anything. Nevertheless, the main line of Plato's philosophical rhetoric pushes toward the attainment of discursive knowledge (*episteme*). We are not to settle for anything less, not the relativism of Protagoras, not the revelations of the mystics, not the voice of traditional authority. We will follow the *logos* of the argument wherever it may lead. Unfortunately, no argument will take us where a cross-strand of Plato's philosophical rhetoric would lead us.

In Plato's dialogues philosophical arguments stop short of *episteme*. We may have adequate discursive knowledge of mud as a mixture of earth and water,[20] but when it comes to anything of moral or intellectual value our ignorance is profound. Socratic dialectic has a tendency to be self-defeating. We search for definitions, become more proficient at coming up with better and better definitions, but we never come up with the final one. We are always at least one step away from our goal.

What we find is that Socrates himself, like the rest of us, must content himself with those beliefs which have withstood the tests of time, experience, and critical reflection. In the *Crito*, for example, Socrates tells his friend that they would be silly if they now abandoned the principles which had stood them in good stead for the whole of their lives.[21] In the *Gorgias* Socrates avows himself "bound in chains of adamant" to his principle that it is better to suffer than to do injustice.[22] To act at all requires that we have confidence in our well-founded beliefs. Socrates asks only that the beliefs upon which we act should be well founded and pass the best tests we can devise for them in dialectical questioning.

The problem is that the demand for *episteme* cannot be met by belief, no matter how well founded that belief may be. We are told that knowledge and belief are different. So it would seem that the best that rational discussion can do is to criticize our beliefs. It cannot provide us with knowledge. Rational arguments fail us at crucial points in our investigation. It is mistaken to think that they will take us all the way. At his most optimistic, Plato has Socrates describe the vision of the Good.[23] Whatever this vision may be, it is not the deductive conclusion of a straightforward philosophical argument. Logic fails us and something else takes over. The theory of recollection falls into place as a strand of philosophical rhetoric which calls the mainline perlocutionary argument into question. The philosophical myth of the Forms and the story of recollection tell against the dominant line which pushes for rational analytic thought. The Forms are not candidates for rational analysis, nor is knowledge of them purely discursive.

Myth shows us the weakness of philosophical argument. Philosophical argument shows us the incompleteness of myth. Faced with philosophical argument, mythical thought acquires the ironic detachment necessary to appreciate its own incompleteness. Faces with the imaginative abundance of myth and poetry, philosophical thought becomes conscious of its own attenuated existence.

A sense of irony is required for the growth of self-knowledge about the practice of poetry and the practice of philosophy. Mythical and philosophical thought hold themselves in abstraction from one another, but only at the cost of diminishing self-consciousness. Forgetful of poetry, philosophy forgets itself, and vice versa. What Plato's dialogues show is how self-contained positions reveal their limitations under pressure, how hidden contradictions come to light. This process is the coming into being of self-knowledge.

Let us take up philosophical positions but be clear about their limitations. Socratic dialectic is the way in which these limitations become the object of an ironic self-consciousness which dissociates itself from its own unthinking project and enters a drama of ideas. Plato's explicit pronouncements do not tell the whole story. The problems with rational arguments, their limitations and weaknesses, emerge just as clearly as those with myth and poetry. We are to recollect this as we move through the positions once again and embrace neither one nor the other without reservations or without the ironic knowledge of both sides' self-subversion. The humor in this situation is not lost on Plato and his jokes have a philosophical punch-line. To understand them is to move in the direction of self-knowledge. But that movement is a perlocutionary effect of Plato's dialogues, a hope on his part, and not the illocutionary effect of his philosophical arguments alone.

It turns out then, that Plato is a poet, a rhetorician, and a philosopher wrapped in one very uneasy bundle. The philosopher totally and seriously committed to analytic reason and clear straightforward thinking wants to exclude poetry and rhetoric to advance his or her own claims. The poet and the rhetor fight the exclusion by claiming their own exclusive rights. It is a tragedy as well as a comedy. Both sides have their own claims, well supported in their own terms but unsupported in the terms of the others. Yet they find themselves inseparably linked in practice once philosophy comes on the scene. Many of the criticisms leveled at opposing views have bite and none of the participants escape unscathed.

Plato writes dialogues, tells stories and myths, employs irony, metaphor, and many other tropes. He is a tropical philosopher. It matters that we are faced with philosophy in a dramatic setting. The drama of Socrates' life and death gives urgency and weight to his words. We are continually brought back to the dilemmas of Socrates' life and work within an existing *polis*. His problems are rooted in the society within which he move¬ and we are never completely allowed to forget it.

Most philosophical writing is different from this. For example, in Aristotle we find an altogether different temperament at work. Where Plato's dialogues are wonderfully written, witty, and amusing, Aristotle's philosophical prose is wooden and pedestrian. Aristotle is not trying to be flashy. He writes in a very compressed and elliptical style (as befits lecture notes) and does not set his philosophy in a dramatic setting. The tenor of his writing is one of dispassionate prose, as clearly and precisely set out as the subject matter permits. His dialectic involves the careful sifting of the best which has been said or written on some topic. We are to weed out contradictions, unfounded remarks, and exaggerations, and keep the best of what is left. In that way we should arrive at a balanced opinion which takes into account what has gone before.

Aristotle is not easy to follow, but the outline of his philosophy is fairly clear. It is marked by the grand polarities of his system: matter and form, actuality and potentiality, virtue and vice, activity and passivity. Include the four causes, and it is possible to sketch out Aristotle's philosophy in rough draft. He argues carefully and sets out his arguments in such a way that we can pick them apart and leisurely examine his premises, conclusions, and logic. All this makes of philosophy a very sober business indeed. Aristotle's philosophical rhetoric aims to make us partners in it.

A common story about Aristotle is that he wrote so beautifully that he acquired the epithet "golden throated." Unfortunately for us, this writing belonged to his exoteric popular work, not the esoteric doctrine which we possess. Nevertheless, attentive readers of Aristotle will note that his writing is not entirely free of poetic and rhetorical devices. Aristotle, too, has an indirect argument to promote, though it is not as pronounced or flamboyant as Plato's. He is trying to get us to see the world in a certain way, and he does that by repeatedly using the metaphor of the organism to help us comprehend the cosmos as a whole.

Aristotle is not the poet Plato is, but that does not mean he does not use poetic resources to make his perlocutionary points. How does the metaphor of the organism work? Think of a living organism. What we notice is that though the organism is articulated into parts, these parts are interanimated and not haphazardly thrown together. The more we examine an organism the more we see how each part performs its function in the life of the whole. No part can perform its function if it is separate from the whole.

The universe is an intelligent organism. This is the metaphor which informs all the abstruse reasoning of Aristotle's physics, metaphysics, his ethics, politics, and aesthetics. It is used to make links between the small world of humans, other animals, and plants to the vast cosmos itself. The problem is that there is no

117

discursive link between the large and the smaller view. Only a metaphor can bridge that gap by endlessly suggesting parallels.

A phenomenon very similar to this is happening much closer to home. It may help us to understand the crucial role of metaphor in the generation and dissemination of philosophical discourse. Consider "The human mind (brain) is a computer." In effect this metaphor is a research project waiting to be started. The brain is the hardware, the mind is the software. Presumably we could design a computer with hardware so like the brain and software so like the mind that we would have nothing to distinguish it from the real thing. We would then have created a machine which can think as we do. Reasoning such as this immediately suggests the project of trying to build intelligent machines which emerge as like humans in their behavior as our programming ability permits.

A good metaphor is bursting with suggestions and hints to be taken up and followed by the person who contemplates it. Up to now the results of the hot computer metaphor of the mind have been disappointing, but there have been results, none the less. We now have computers which can discriminate between simple shapes and colors. There are talking computers that recognize a restricted vocabulary and a precise grammar. Computers are programmed to perform actions imitative of human actions.

The problem comes when, after the first flush of metaphorical enthusiasm, we start to take our metaphor literally. The death of a metaphor is the birth of a dogma. In the present case we come to something like this: "The mind (brain) is a digital computer." This is much less suggestive though it arose at the suggestion of the original metaphor. We know too much about digital computers. It is false to assert this latter metaphor literally, but its use as a metaphor is minimal. What are we to do with it? Perhaps we must rethink the concept of a computer on altogether different lines.

Though the computer metaphor of the mind still has some way to run, it is becoming clear that certain avenues of investigation are closing down. The metaphor is running out of juice. As it does, so discussion becomes more and more technical and abstract. The impetus behind the original exploration is lost; the field becomes increasingly barren and is finally abandoned when there is nothing further to do there. If, and when, the computer metaphor of the mind runs out of suggestions for further research, it will be abandoned without much pain or regret by all except the die-hards.

Metaphor and its near relations, simile and analogy, have acquired an extensive bibliography in recent years.[24] The discussions have largely centered upon questions concerning the nature and existence of metaphorical meaning, the distinction between metaphorical and non-metaphorical expressions, whether or not such expressions are parasitic upon basic literal discourse, and so on. I do not intend to address this problem across the whole field. I want to focus on the use of metaphor in philosophical writing. The general theory of metaphor is relevant only in so far as it helps us understand the philosopical use of metaphor, or philosophical poetics.

Sample questions include the following. Does metaphor reveal a meaning which cannot be captured in straightforward prose? Is there such a thing as metaphorical meaning? Do individual words have a literal meaning on the one hand and a metaphorical meaning on the other? These and similar questions have a number of flaws. One is that they are asked in a context fashioned out of preoccupations with the theory of meaning conceived as part of a theory of language. There are prior interests and concerns involved in the asking and the answering of the questions. A number of issues are relevant to our understanding of metaphor in philosophical writing.

In one story the discussion of linguistic meaning is tied to the serious and literal use of language. That is because the concept of truth finds its most immediate employment there. Roughly speaking, we are to determine the meaning of sentences by analyzing their truth conditions. To utter a sentence with truth conditions is to utter a meaningful sentence. We determine the meaning by determining the conditions under which the sentence is true. That is what the sentence means.

This view has the sensible conclusion[25] that there is no such thing as the metaphorical meaning of words. The only meaning which words have is the ordinary one. Metaphor is simply the extraordinary use of expressions and sentences made up of words with their own pedestrian meanings. The meanings remain the same; it is the use made of them that produces metaphor.

The conclusion is sensible in view of the difficulties produced by the alternatives. What is needed here is a minimal description of metaphor, and that is exactly what the sensible account makes available. To argue that there exists, beside the ordinary meaning of words in familiar combinations, a metaphorical meaning which is the "real" meaning of an expression or sentence, invites a number of embarrassing questions.

Let us take the familiar example, "Juliet is the sun." The separatists would hold that though it is not literally true that Juliet is the sun, there is a meaning of "sun" of which it is true to say of Juliet that she is the sun. "Sun" here means, metaphorically, "light of my life" or some other such substitution. The problem is to specify exactly what this metaphorical meaning is. "The light of my life" can be used to explicate the metaphorical "meaning" of "sun" in "Juliet is the sun", but other substitutions are possible. Furthermore, "light of my life" is itself metaphorical and requires explication.

The result is that we are unable to give "the metaphorical meaning" of a term or sentence. We can give different renderings or readings of a metaphor, and metaphors worth their salt take plural readings. They are multivocal, not univocal; suggestive, not definite. This is the excellence of metaphor. It cannot be pinned down and always takes various readings or explications.

In recent years the direction of analytic/linguistic philosophy is in agreement with this point. Black and Davidson, though disagreeing with each other on many issues, agree that an interesting metaphor cannot be paraphrased in non-metaphorical language.[26] Something is always lost in a straightforward rendering of metaphorical language.

Metaphors conceal their meaning or significance at the same time as they reveal it. To pick on one aspect and render it in straightforward prose is to stipulate a fixed meaning for the metaphor. But since the job of a metaphor is to open up a field of interpretation, this "fixing" of the meaning is misguided.

There are at least two strategies for fixing the meaning of a metaphor. One relies upon the interpretative schema through which a metaphor is examined. The other relies upon the intentions of the author. According to the first strategy, the superior status of the interpretative schema employed by the strategist picks out a meaning of the metaphor superior to other contenders. The other more humble approach bases the appropriateness of an interpretation upon something outside the schema of interpretation.

In the latter case, we are to suppose that the metaphor means one thing on the surface and another below the surface. It is the meaning which lies below the surface that is identified with the intention of the author. Therefore, if we could only know enough about the intentions of authors, we could pick out with certainty the real meaning of the metaphors used.

The main problem with this approach is the impossibility of determining the intentions of authors. More serious, however, is the fact that after the production of a text, the author's relation to it is on all fours with that of everyone else. The poet has no privileged access to the "real" meaning of his or her own poetry. It is wrong even to speak of the poet as owning or somehow possessing a poem he or she has written. At most, the poet can own the copyright.

The effect of metaphor is indirect and perlocutionary and outside the conscious or unconscious intention of the author. Imagine yourself a poet writing the line "Juliet is the sun." You may have a number of interpretations in mind, and find the line is apt to produce them in the mind of the reader or hearer. That is a good enough reason for using the line, but it does not exhaust its meaning. Metaphors spark thoughts in a number of different directions. A good metaphor produces unexpected effects. The poet transcends himself or herself in the metaphors created. The reader or audience must complete the metaphor, giving it an interpretation based on an already held interpretative schema.

To borrow a term from philosophical logic, we could say that metaphors are unsaturated. They require an argument, so to speak, to be completed. A poet may indeed complete his or her own metaphors, just as anyone else may. As with rhetoric, the effect of metaphors will depend upon the audience's responses to them. What these may be can never be foreclosed by the metaphor itself, and thus lie outside the author's intentions in writing.

Much the same can be said for the former strategy which relies upon the superiority of one's interpretative schema to dig out the "real" or "best" interpretation of the metaphor. One problem is to determine exactly what the best interpretative schema is. A more serious problem is that the assertion of "the meaning" of a metaphor falsifies the basic nature of the metaphor, which is to be open to interpretation in the first place. No amount of "spelling out" can exhaust the suggestiveness of the metaphor without destroying it. A dead metaphor is simply a metaphor routinely interpreted in fixed ways so that its suggestiveness is lost.

A living metaphor resonates with multiple and sometimes incompatible meanings. There is always the chance that a changing response will produce understandings very different to those which have become standard. Metaphor is the source of novelty in our changing conceptual network. The novelty produced is not that of any of the conceptual renderings of the metaphor. It is rather in the invitation to look in unforeseen directions. Philosophical metaphors in particular act as guides which point out places of interest and scenic trails which follow a particular route through the philosophical landscape. We are invited to look out from those places and take the suggested trails. If, like the computer metaphor of the mind, the places pointed out and the trails recommended by the metaphor seem promising and the analogies instructive, the metaphor will motivate us to investigate the world in certain ways. It is up to us to do it.

The use of metaphorical language in philosophy is part of its philosophical rhetoric, part of its strategy for producing not just changes in beliefs, but also in emotions, desires, and feelings. These cannot be accomplished through straightforward rational argument. Whether some desire is taken up or some feeling felt, the cooperation and skill of the audience are required. It is hard for a rational mind to refuse the conclusion of a sound argument. The heart has no such scruples. Philosophical argument has never persuaded anyone to change his or her ways unless the desire to change them is already active. Strict philosophical argument is only part of the process of rational persuasion.

As a test case, consider the old chestnut about whether the mind is innately endowed with ideas. The way into this problem is not directly through the arguments, but through the metaphors which figure in them. There are at least two metaphors which stand out as guides to philosophical thinking about innate ideas. One is Locke's famous "blank slate,"[27] the other is Leibniz's "block of marble."[28]

Let us first explore the metaphor of the "blank slate": "the mind is a blank slate." We can be fairly certain that this is a metaphor. If we take it literally, then it is either false or not a candidate for truth or falsity. So it must be something else, a metaphor. We are to start looking for analogies. Slate is a flat black rock upon which it is possible to write with chalk. A blank slate is one which has yet to be written on. Furthermore, the slate itself is passive. It does not write on itself, but sits blank until written upon. The slate is indifferent to what is written upon it. There are no invisible characters already inscribed upon a blank slate; its blankness eliminates that possibility.

These considerations are now brought into connection with our thoughts about the human mind. Perhaps we had never thought of linking them before, but if we do, a number of interesting parallels appear. "The mind is a blank slate." This means that, like a slate, the mind is a passive receptor of inscriptions. Some power external to the mind imprints it with those sensations which furnish it with contents. The mind, therefore, contains no ideas before it is imprinted from without. Hence it has no innate ideas.

At this point the metaphor is left behind in pursuit of the argument, but it still informs the whole orientation of the project of philosophical inquiry which Locke proposes. The metaphor of the "blank slate" is part of his perlocutionary argument for the "empirical" perspective in philosophy.

Locke is trying to get us to realize that there is a passive dimension to the mind. The metaphor of the slate works quite well here, presenting us with a vivid and memorable picture to which we can fix this idea. However, when we continue to expand and articulate the metaphor, it begins to break down.

One large difference between the mind and a blank slate is that the mind is conscious of itself but the slate is not. The way Locke has it, sensations are produced in us through causal interaction with a material world which is other than mind. We are thus dependent upon those interactions to produce in us the materials of thought and experience. Without them the mind remains merely a blank slate. At the same time, however, Locke affirms that the mind does, after all, have certain powers or capacities to reflect upon the sensations provided by causal interaction with the external world. We can compare ideas together, pick out similarities and differences, and we are aware that we are doing this. Pieces of rock are not aware of anything. The mind has a native endowment of specific capacities which channel and shape the incoming sensations. The mind is active, after all, and not passive as the metaphor implies.

Locke is not easy to understand at all points in his argument and he says different things at different times. Nevertheless, he does grant the mind powers which are not found in slates.

The use of this metaphor in Locke's philosophical rhetoric acts as a focus and catalyst for thinking through previously unthought conceptual connections. It is not a last word. The use of metaphor in philosophy marks the beginning of an inquiry, not the end. When we have worked through Locke's argument we can always go back and look at the metaphor with which we started and see that it is, after all, only a metaphor. But it is a powerful one which has a place in the common stock of philosophical metaphors. It sums up certain aspects of the mind which it is in the interest of Locke's philosophical rhetoric to emphasize.

Let us turn to Leibniz's counter metaphor: "innate ideas are the veins in a block of marble." Ideas are innate to the mind as the grain of the marble is to the sculptor's block of stone. Leibniz's metaphor is more complicated than Locke's. We are to see the mind as a block of stone, and experience as the chisel which shapes it. The sculptor's block of stone is passive in the sense that it, too, waits for the sculptor's hand to give it shape. But unlike the slate, the block has its own character built into it. Long before any of the stone is chipped away, its grain is there. The end result of the sculptor's work is the combination of what was in the stone already and chip marks left by the chisel. The sculptor reveals what is already in the stone at the same time as creating a shape.

Innate ideas are not little pictures in the mind, but the mind's structure and power. We are created to receive confused perceptions in a certain way; our minds are structured to work in a certain manner. Talk of innate ideas is simply a way of bringing this out. The metaphor of the block of marble is part of a strategy to make us think of the mind in a certain way, to visualize its internal structure. It provides us with a focus and catalyst for our reflections on the nature of the mind, but takes us in different directions from those suggested by Locke's metaphor of the blank slate.

Just as the veins in the marble are laid bare by the sculptor's chisel, so the catalyst of experience activates innate capacities in us. We are not born with a self-conscious knowledge of the laws of logic, but should we ever reflect on them, our conclusions will match those of people who have made a study of them. The metaphor of the block of marble works to make our understanding of a very general and abstract topic more concrete. Yet it, too, has weaknesses if pressed too far. The image of a block of stone is a passive one, and yet, for Leibniz, mind is wholly active. Nothing can act upon anything else in the sense of exerting an outside force. There are no outside forces. All relations between substances are internal relations. The so-called external world of objects in space and time is the result of our finite intelligences working with confused, though well founded, perceptions.

Perhaps God is the sculptor. How does the metaphor work then? First, we must recall that Leibniz's God creates the best of all possible worlds out of the infinitely many possibilities guaranteed by logic. How is that like a sculptor chipping off bits of stone? Can we see Leibniz's universe of monads as a whole stone and the exclusion of the other possible worlds as the chippings? We might be able to push this analogy a bit further, but it is already strained. It is hard to find an analogy between concepts which arise through the confused perceptions available to our senses, such as "block of stone," and the individual substances (monads) which populate Leibniz's universe. Individual substances are logically basic but imperceptible to the senses. Their nature is that of a *vis viva*, or active force, whose substance lies outside the phenomenal world of the senses. The analogy between mind and stone breaks down.

Nevertheless, the stone metaphor does serve a purpose. It crystallizes, in a not totally satisfactory way, the concept of internal structure. Like Aristotle, Leibniz is attracted to the metaphor of the organism as a way of orientating himself to phenomena. The problem with the block of marble metaphor is that it does not fit very well with the overriding metaphor of organism. Our concept of a rock, which we derive from perception, is not the concept of an organic being. Yet it is used to help us to focus on the mind as an organic being having an internal structure. It is important to Leibniz that we should do this since, for him, internal structure is the key to a thing's being what it is.

For Locke, on the contrary, knowledge which comes to us through experience, not pure thought, is to govern our thinking and investigations. He is not attracted to the organic metaphor of the universe. We live in a world which is not of our making, which is other than we are, and which affects us in various ways. The causal story Locke tells to account for our experiences is part of this point. In Locke's account it is the metaphor of the mechanism which is to draw our attention and investigation. Locke's metaphor of the blank slate which is written on from without draws attention to the causal dependency of the human mind. The production of ideas in us is the result of causal processes which work through the mechanism of our bodies, not through a wholly internal principle. Locke is not a mechanist *tout court*, but he encourages the investigation suggested by the metaphor of the machine.[29]

Locke and Leibniz match metaphors as well as arguments. We have looked at the "blank slate" and the "block of marble," the "machine" and the "organism." There are more. I suspect, however, that the majority of them use the same perlocutionary argument as the dominant philosophical rhetoric of their respective approaches to philosophy.

Locke comes across in his philosophical writings as a no-nonsense, down-to-earth sort of thinker who will not tolerate the excesses of philosophical speculation. He presents himself as the humble under-laborer of science.[30] He says he is content merely to tidy up the conceptual field, and to prevent muddles and verbal enthusiasms. He is a sensible man calling out to the common sense in each of us. He is not pretentious. He uses metaphors sparingly and only when he has to. Critical of rhetoric, he speaks as plainly as the subject matter allows. Let us just sit down and discuss things as rational beings. We will find that if we define our terms, stick to those things of which we have experience, and employ a rational method, we will agree at least on the broad outline of the truth to be sought and the means to find it. In this way we shall be spared the excesses of shoddy thinking and ill-considered enthusiasms.

Though Locke uses metaphors sparingly and could hardly be called a poet, the indirection of his argument leads him to use them, none the less. One problem with writing philosophy in a climate of contention is that it is necessary to create one's audience at the same time as one states the argument of the case. In Austin's terms, one must secure "uptake."[31] The philosopher who would be heard must somehow capture the attention of the audience. Neither Locke nor any other philosophical writer can escape this fact. The resources of poetry and rhetoric aid in the task of securing an audience.

Whether used sparingly or copiously, metaphors are crucial to the mix of indirect techniques which work to make an audience receptive to the philosophical message explicit in the text. They do this by opening the mind of the audience to new combinations of ideas, fields of meaning hitherto unthought or inaccessible. The metaphors which have been discussed all stick in the mind because they do just this. Each opens up a field of meaning or significance which has implications for the ways in which we see and understand the world. The metaphor opens up an angle of vision and thus functions as an invitation to change perspectives. It is vital that the invitation be taken up if a shift of philosophical stance is required to advance the argument.

On the whole it is correct to say that the words of a language have the meaning that they do outside of a metaphorical context. There is a rough and ready sense of "literal meaning" which it makes very little sense to contest. The meanings of the words in "Juliet is the sun" are the same as those in, for example, "Juliet is a character in one of Shakespeare's plays" or "The sun is eight light-minutes from the earth." What makes an expression metaphorical is not its literal falsity, but the lack of fit of the terms related. Literally, the sun is whatever the current position of astrophysics tells us. Characters in plays are not discussed in astrophysics. We are baffled. The normal inferences and expectations do not go through. We are stopped by a metaphor because all of a sudden we are faced with indeterminacy of meaning.

"Juliet is the sun." What can this possibly mean? An active metaphor elicits interpretation and the production of meanings. Ideas are linked together which normally we would not think of contemplating together. Thus the use of metaphors acts as a kind of catalyst upon the audience which brings about a change in thinking. It is part of an indirect strategy to bring the audience to a way of thinking, writing, and talking which is the effect of a perlocutionary argument, "argued" indirectly through the use of tropes and other devices. Changes in philosophical understanding are accompanied by changes in attitude brought about in large part through indirect means. Metaphor is a conspicuous example.

As long as philosophical speech and writing appear in rhetorical settings, as long as it is necessary to engage in polemical debates, philosophical productions will contain a philosophical rhetoric. It is difficult to prove this assertion either a priori or a posteriori. It is difficult to prove it a posteriori because it is a matter of looking at examples of philosophical writing to see whether they contain evidence of their own rhetoric, either self-consciously and iron-ically, or unconsciously and naïvely. The field of philosophical production is not a closed one. Not everything has been said in it. The best we can do is look backward at the texts we know and see if we can find some indications of philosophical rhetoric at work. I think we can; and we have yet to see a philosophical production which bypasses philosophical rhetoric. At best this is a true empirical generalization. A counter-example may emerge.

As for the argument a priori, that goes against the intuition that a counter-example may indeed make an appearance. It does not seem to be self-contradictory to suppose that a philosophy could present itself as without rhetoric, poetic tropes or any kind of mystification. Many different systems of philosophy have been presented in just this way. Nevertheless, the philosophical rhetoric can be worked out in each case by the attentive observer. The problem with the notion of a rhetoric-free philosophy cannot be settled on a priori grounds. Yet there is a problem, and I suggest that the problem lies in a failure of the imagination to picture a world in which rhetoric-free philosophy might exist.

Try to imagine such a world. For a start, it would require the disappearance of the whole academic establishment. It would be the end of professional philosophers, of journals, honors, awards, tenure, conditions of working. A way of life would vanish. Competition would end, no more polemics against favored opponents, no more attempts to get other people to see the world in a certain way or to act in a certain way. We reach rhetoric degree zero.

This is hard enough to imagine. It is even harder to try to imagine a world in which philosophical discourse does not make use of metaphor. I am using "metaphor" to stand for metaphor, simile, and analogy, the whole field in which different things are brought together and compared which cannot literally be brought together and compared. Can we imagine a philosophical writing which excluded all metaphor and analogy? Perhaps we can. Perhaps a logical philosophy which proceeded axiomatically could be expressed, but this would be a highly truncated conception of philosophy. What would be the point of setting it out? Outside of a rhetorical situation, however minimal, what is the motivation to communicate or make signs?

Even the most business-like writings in philosophical logic find themselves obliged to take polemical sides in an argument, make metaphors and analogies (all the while apologizing for having to use them), and generally set the stage for the serious business of the work. You will often find them at the beginning of the work, in the preface or introduction. You will find them in places marginalized by the main channel of philosophical argument.

The language of philosophical logic is a form of rhetorical "plain style" which originated in the reformation of rhetoric from within.[32] To be schooled in the traditions of "conceptual analysis" or "ordinary language" is to be schooled in rhetoric as well, though it is never taught as such. The standards of acceptable philosophical prose, I remember, emphasized a clear, plain style based on the precise (not to say punctilious) use of language. The *topos* of rhetoric was never an explicitly recognized theme.

Once we understand the "plain style" of speaking or writing as a rhetorical style, it becomes easier to recognize the rhetoric of even the barest style of writing. The writings of philosophical logic display this plain style and avoid the conspicuous use of metaphor and rhetoric. They are characterized by a lack of those very devices. This lack itself functions as a rhetorical-cum-philosophical device which produces perlocutionary effects in a range far exceeding any which the proponents of a philosophical logic might intend.

We may express this as a directive coming from the investigation of formal logic itself: shun the metaphorical. Aim for explicitness. Every sign in a logical language has a meaning uniquely determining and determined by the range of its uses in the language. We can tell the difference between well-formed formulas and those which are not well formed. It is a question of syntax. The context of well-formed formulas is universal. Its only interest is in the logical relations which hold between them. Any proposition which is a candidate for truth must first pass the preliminary interview with logic. Formal logic may not be able to tell us anything true about the world, but it does tell us the form which a candidate for truth must have.

Metaphorical sentences are not well formed. They bring an element of indeterminacy with which the logical machinery is not designed to cope. A metaphor could mean this, or it could mean that. In either case, the terms involved look very little like the signs of a logical language. Ordinary language itself does not function as a logical language, and straightforward linguistic communications often contain ambiguities which cannot be tolerated in formal logic. Such language is peppered with metaphors now taken for granted, idiomatic expressions, and the vagueness demanded by casual conversation and utilitarian communication.

Aristotle's dictum that we should pursue that degree of precision which is allowed for by our topic[33] applies across the board. Language is open-textured and will accommodate a wide latitude of usage. In the area of utilitarian communication something very like Grice's maxims of conversation come into play.[34] One of these states that when giving information, give neither too little nor too much. It would be absurd for me to give you a step-by-step itinerary of the way to the nearest library if I could simply say, "Turn left at the next intersection and it will be on your right." To the list of maxims for straightforward communication we might add, "Keep your metaphors down to a minimum." Metaphors break up the transparency of the communication. When what we want is efficiency of transmission of information, metaphors disrupt the transmission lines. Extraneous meaning enters in. Efficiency is lost. We want our information short and to the point, not too much, not too little. We want the maximum of compression without loss of explicitness.

This point of view makes sense if we restrict ourselves to straightforward instrumental communication. In that context we do not want to waste words. After all, it is the result which is important, not the means of arriving at it. I suspect that one of the main reasons for the tendency to think that prose language is transparent is the suppressed premise of instrumental communication. For if we suppose that to be the context of utterance or inscription, then language itself fades into the background. When language does call attention to itself and gives us pause, it is because something is wrong.

However, when we see language operate outside of a straightforward instrumental context, as we do when contemplating the philosophical tropes, what is an obstruction in the transmission line and completely marginal comes to be of focal interest. Metaphors open up new semantic fields through indirection. The metaphor suggests, hints, implies, indicates, points, and so on, but it does not come right out and say anything. If language use is judged from the point of view that saying something is the whole function of speech or writing, then metaphors and other indirect devices are bound to disappoint. The success or failure of a metaphor is so indeterminable and so dependent upon the whim of the audience, that it cannot serve as a vehicle of discursive knowledge (*episteme*). Discursive knowledge is that which is captured in straightforward, non-metaphorical prose, and it does not depend upon the audience for more than a knowledge of the language which they both speak.

This is fine as far as it goes, but it is a pity to stop with the field of instrumental communication. Poetry severs the instrumental links of ordinary language and creates a semantic space in which there is room for the free play of imagination on the part of the audience. This is no doubt distracting if there is something more urgent to do. In that case, dreaming is a bit beside the point. But in other contexts it may be precisely the point.

If I am right, indirect communication is ruled out by the assumption of primacy of the domain of straightforward instrumental communication. What we saw in the case of rhetoric occurs again. With the restriction in place, philosophy allies itself with an unconscious rhetoric of the "plain style," but there is no acknowledgment of old debts to the rhetorical tradition of antiquity and the Renaissance.

We have seen that in the case of anti-rhetorical philosophical writing the problem is that the rhetorician can employ indirect means to further particular ends. A certain indirection is always possible. It is instrumental in this limited sense that oratory is produced to influence people in their beliefs and actions. Yet even anti-rhetorical philosophical writing is produced to influence belief and action. Though its rhetoric is very low key, it is very strict about what is proper. There will be no unseemly rhetorical display.

The logical writings have a rhetoric which is like minimalism in modern art. There is a definite display of a very bare conceptual repertoire. What both logic and minimalist painting have in common is the creation of empty spaces. This is not meant to be said in disparagement of either logic or minimalist art. There is something expansive about both of them. Logic gives us a world bounded only by formal contradiction. Minimalist art gives us a visual world bounded only by ever receding horizons. The "rhetoric" of minimalist art and philosophical logic leaves a well-defined trail for those who wish to read the signs. They both take up a well-defined stance in their respective worlds. There is something minimally pleasing about the austere rhetoric. For someone with the right intellectual talents and a suitable frame of mind, bare rhetoric will be just the right thing and the game goes on. The commonplaces on which it proceeds are perpetuated by the activity of producing philosophical writings of this logical type.

Philosophical writing is tropical. The philosophical rhetoric of the logical variety of anti-rhetorical philosophy writing is very pared down, low key, self-effacing and stern. It is a minimalist rhetoric. Not all philosophical rhetorics are like this. We have already examined quite a few. I argue that philosophical writing can do as little without metaphor as without a persuasive rhetoric. The two are closely connected since the use of a metaphor is part of the overall perlocutionary argument of the writing. Metaphor is a way of winning the audience over, making the audience more susceptible to the truth of what is always proved elsewhere. Where the audience is already won over, the need for metaphor is greatly reduced. One does not expect a poetry recital when attending a colloquium on sense and reference in Frege and Kripke. A great body of background knowledge and interest is assumed without reflection. The whole discussion makes no sense to someone who is not familiar with the techniques of formal logic and the kinds of discussions which surround its main topics.

However, we cannot make such assumptions about philosophical writings situated outside a clearly defined field. Metaphor comes into its own as a way of establishing links with a partly unknown audience. Philosophical metaphors are access routes to a field of investigation. They are left behind once the place of investigation is reached. However, this "place" is the place of the professional philosopher. Can one imagine a more professional group than the one which regularly participates in the production and consumption of writing in the field of philosophical logic? Professors, graduate students, publishing houses, universities, degrees, awards, research grants, and more, all come together to support the specialized knowledge displayed so excellently in colloquia on topics of philosophical logic.

The minimalist philosophical rhetoric represented here is not the only possible one. It is not the only style of writing we find. If I were a minimalist about philosophical rhetoric, I would be positively embarrassed by the writing of some of my so-called fellow philosophers. For example, the writings of Kierkegaard and Nietzsche are so riddled with rhetorical and poetic devices that to call them "philosophical" writings is euphemistic. Yet the more flamboyant rhetoric and poetry of Kierkegaard and Nietzsche are no more or less philosophical rhetoric than the minimalist one of philosophical logic.

From the arctic vistas of minimalist philosophical rhetoric to the tropical jungles of Kierkegaard and Nietzsche, we are dealing with the same phenomena. The philosophers we traditionally think, write, and talk about made significant use of the resources of metaphor. (I am picking on metaphor because I believe that it is central to the production of philosophical arguments.) We find them in the tradition from the pre-Socratics through Plato, Aristotle, and others to Descartes, Spinoza, Leibniz, Hobbes, Locke, Berkeley, Hume, Kant, Fichte, Schelling, Hegel, Schopenhauer, Kierkegaard, Marx, Nietzsche, Freud, Frege, Husserl, and so on. Setting these figures out in this way is already to read that tradition, but they are familiar figures.

It is not as easy to memorize philosophical writings as it is to memorize poetry. Philosophy books are just too big. The arguments are intricate and detailed. There is too much to remember. The text enables us to go back and find out what is written on a certain page. But we can also do it through the main metaphors which are so compressed that they are not useful in straightforward communication. They become valuable as reminders of the places to begin and as suggestions of directions to take.

Philosophical metaphors, by which I mean those with a role to play in philosophical rhetoric, can be "known" in the same privileged way that a poem can be known. "The mind is a blank slate." Think of this line as a bad poem capable of being known, reflected on, and recollected. We can begin to unpack the metaphor in ways which remind us of other things which Locke writes, of the whole setting of his writing, and many other things. Perhaps an analogy will help. Final exams are coming up in plane geometry. Certain things must be memorized, the axioms certainly, and perhaps some handy postulates. There are also a host of theorems which can be memorized. Now if one had a photographic memory it might be easiest to memorize everything, and there would be no problem with the exam. Without such a memory another strategy is called for. Memorize the axioms, familiarize yourself with the methods of geometrical proof, and then derive whatever theorems are needed on the day. Philosophical metaphors are like geometrical axioms from which it is possible to derive the main line of the argument without having a detailed grasp of it in advance.

Philosophical metaphors give us a way to traverse philosophical ground without grinding out the details at every turn. They enable us to find our way about the philosophical landscape. They are vital both in learning to do philosophy and in teaching the subject. But more than that, the metaphors, dicta, fragments, and remembered stories which surround philosophical argument give content and import to the argument itself.

Metaphorical language in philosophical writing is a constant companion to philosophical argument. Through metaphor the place of argument is made accessible. Consider the classic metaphor which Hume uses to discuss causality, the billiard ball example.[35] It is so vivid that I suspect it is one of the last things a casual student of Hume forgets. It is all there with a little imagination: the logical distinction between cause and effect, priority in time, contiguity in space, constant conjunction, and repeatability. Given the metaphor, it is almost possible to work out a priori what is involved in Hume's theory of causation. All we have to do is examine the picture he paints of the behavior of billiard balls on a table.

So far this is the picture of causality Hume wishes us to have. We are to think about purely mechanical push-pull operations. Are they not all exactly like the effects of billiard balls impacting on one another? We learn by experience what to expect of future events by understanding what consequences regularly follow from occurrences of a particular kind. We find that imparting a certain direction and velocity to the cue ball regularly leads to the object ball's disappearance into the side pocket. To speak this way is to go with the grain of Hume's philosophical rhetoric. We are meant to recognize the lack of necessity in what we call "causation" and to accept it as a fact about our psychology, not about things-in-themselves.

Metaphors like this are janus-faced. On the one hand, Hume's metaphor invites a certain interpretation both of it and of causation. On the other hand, there are interpretations which belong on the guest list but never get their invitations. Hume's metaphor gives us a vivid picture of what the world of causal interactions is like. It shows the place where we can look and find what we are looking for. But at the same time it discourages interpretations which would apply another principle of explanation. For example, it makes sense to say that we have stated what water is when we have explained that it is made up of water molecules which stand in predictable relations to each other at specific temperatures and pressures. The liquid you see before you consists of the water molecules which make it up behaving together as they do at room temperature. The micro-structures of water molecules in combination is the cause of the global features of water which our senses detect.[36]

It seems possible that Hume's metaphor, while fulfilling its role in his philosophical rhetoric, forecloses a little too neatly upon other options such as structural causation. Hume's primary trope is metonymy, not metaphor. Metonymy is the trope of contingency and conventional association. In fact, anything at all can join two terms in a metonymical relation. For example, if we speak of the boot of despotism crushing the people under its heel, there is a metonymical relation to the action of a person who holds unaccountable power. In my imagination I see the boots of a military dictator. The association is arbitrary and conventional. But it would work just as well in a world where military dictators wear tennis shoes. Then we would have another metonymy: the tennis shoe of despotism. These are the sort of relations Hume likes, those between logically separate individuals.

To break with the Humean metaphor of causality we need another one to put in its place. Instead of the transitive temporality of Hume's metaphor, we need one which is transtemporal. What is wanted is something like the explanatory scheme Aristotle discussed under the heading of *formal causation*. If x is the formal cause of y, it does not follow that x preceeds y in time, or that x and y can enter into contiguous relations in space. For example, the computer program which is directing the computer to operate as a simple word processor is the formal cause of the word processing function of the computer. Before the first word is written down the word processor must be functioning properly. It is functioning properly when the program does its job of directing the computer to perform certain operations. There is no sense in which the program comes before the word-processing function of the computer as one moving billiard ball comes before another one.

One metaphor which suggests itself is *structure*. The structure of a thing is not something which can either precede it or come into contiguous relation to it. Hume's billiard ball metaphor rules out a structural explanation which has as much right to be entitled "causal" as any other.

The metaphor of structure suggests an analogy with building. A building is a construction. It is made up of parts which fit together within a structural integrity. We can, in partial abstraction, speak of the structure of the building. What we call a blueprint is just such a partial abstraction. The blueprint gives us the structural outline.

Consider the difference in perception between an architect and a lay person in the appreciation of a construction. In a very concrete sense, the architect makes informed judgments about the structural features of the building which are not part of the global vision accessible to untrained sight. I cannot see the reinforced concrete in the building before me unless I already know it is there. Looking at the blueprint I can, as it were, peel back the concrete and expose the iron within. The building becomes a system of systems. There is the heating system, the ventilation system, the plumbing system, the wiring system, the floor-plan system, and all the others which architects coordinate in their blueprints. Each will have a synchronic structural explanation which gives the formal causes of the respective systems.

The switch from diachrony in Hume's metaphor of metonymy to synchrony in the metaphor of structure marks a *Gestalt* switch, a perlocutionary effect of looking in the directions indicated by the respective metaphors. To look in the directions indicated by the metaphor of structure opens up new fields of relevance. It is a very different thing to look at the universe as if it were some kind of giant clockwork mechanism, or to see it as a structure. The imperatives of structuralism are different from those of mechanism.

Let us try to look at everything as if it had structure. How far can we go with this idea? We need not rehearse the convoluted history of structuralism, but it is certain that the metaphor of structure has proved suggestive of a number of lines of research. These have revealed structural explanations of varying degrees of cogency, but plainly we can go quite a way down structural lines before the rewards of the investigation cease to be worth the effort.

Metaphors do break down and hence show their status as metaphors. But their job is not to stand up to all criticism but to suggest modes of perception and inquiry to be taken up and followed. To ask a metaphor to do more than this, to ask it to be literally true and worked out to completeness, is to ask too much. The fact that "post-structuralism" follows "structuralism" simply attests to the breakdown of the primary metaphor. We cannot literally apply structuralist principles to anything whatsoever with equal effect. Some topics lend themselves to structuralist analysis. Others do not. The point of the metaphor, however, is to open up a field of relevance which can then be exploited to varying degrees of success. The best metaphors are very prolific in the production of interesting and stimulating suggestions. As long as it remains open to interpretation and expansion, a metaphor feeds energy into the philosophical arguments which it stimulates. A metaphor that becomes formulaic and is given a fixed interpretation loses its vitality; that is, it ceases to be productive of those perlocutionary effects on which its life as a metaphor depends.

It would be interesting to have a study on the major metaphors of western philosophical writing. I have been able to discuss only a few. My aim, however, is not to make a survey of philosophical metaphors, but to show that philosophical writing continually makes use of them as part of its philosophical rhetoric. I would like to conclude this chapter with a brief discussion of three bird metaphors and their relation to the philosophical rhetoric of three philosophers. I call it the philosophers' aviary. There is Locke's sparrow,[37] Kant's dove,[38] and Hegel's owl.[39] Let us take them in order.

Locke does not take a respectful attitude to birds. He is a hunter, but a modest one. He is going out not after eagles, but sparrows. He is going to aim at what he has a chance to hit and finds quite enough sport in that. He leaves the big birds to the speculative metaphysicians. Locke's metaphor fits into a philosophical rhetoric which pushes toward a no-nonsense, down-to-earth attitude to knowledge and experience. The reader picks this up indirectly through the metaphor by imaginatively picturing the scene of philosophical activity as that of hunting small game. The sparrows are those little problems and confusions which the philosopher might just be able to clear up a little.

Kant's dove fares better than the poor sparrows which Locke busily hunts for sport, yet it performs a similar function in his philosophical rhetoric. We are to imagine Kant's dove flying through the air, its natural element. It is not a target for hunters. But Kant's dove is a dreamer and dreams to itself that it would be so much nicer to soar through the sky without the drag of air resistance holding it back. How much better it would be to fly above the atmosphere. The dove is a dreamer because it does not reflect on the fact that if it were not for air resistance, it would not be able to fly at all. Kant's dove does not have to stay right on the ground, but it cannot get too far away. The dove is a metaphor for the speculation which would free itself of the resistance caused by our empirical existence. Kant's philosophical rhetoric aims through the image to bring about the end of craving for what is beyond our capacities to attain. But this is an indirect result of Kant's metaphor, and one which, therefore, depends upon the response of the audience.

Hegel's owl is a very different bird from the others. The first two enjoin us to take a commonplace attitude to our investigations into knowledge. The owl is part of a different philosophical rhetoric. It invites us to take a certain perspective on history and thought not suggested by the other bird metaphors.

Hegel's owl, of course, is the owl of Minerva. We are told it only flies at twilight. There is no question here of hunting it or advising it to stay in the earthly air. Rather, Hegel speaks of the owl as of philosophy itself. Taking wing in the evening, the owl surveys the results of the day with no thought for the morrow. Like an owl, philosophy takes flight only after the world it seeks to understand has already been formed. The owl is a metaphor for the backward looking endeavor of philosophical investigation. The owl is a symbol of knowledge and second sight. It is a bird of memory.

Hegel's philosophical rhetoric produces that recollection in his audience which will liberate it from all one-sided thinking. Hegel wants us to let go of all our most cherished illusions and yet remember them for what they are, constitutive elements of the experience under review.

In the Introduction to the *Phenomenology* Hegel makes it clear that he wants his reader to drop the demand for complete satisfaction in any position covered. Philosophical theories are not like candies which one either buys or does not buy. They are partial expressions of a truth which transcends every position, but which cannot be encapsulated in one. Hegel uses philosophical metaphors to capture at a glance the perspectives of the different

138

mental formations which revolve through the gallery of *Geist*.

A metaphor is a kind of shorthand which enables us to put complicated concepts into motion. The metaphor of the owl calls up both the powers and liabilities of philosophical thought. Philosophical thought comes to grips with the in-itself, but only as it was. The being which thought determines is already fixed by history and has its meaning there. Hegel makes no more than the vaguest statements about the future direction of history.

If Hegel's metaphors come into play to fix in our minds positions which will not ultimately survive "scientific" scrutiny, then we can make sense of Hegel's drive toward a thoroughly conceptual prose, which passes beyond the "picture-thinking" of metaphor.[40]

Hegel has a particularly virulent strain of anti-rhetorical philosophical rhetoric.[41] The role of metaphor in it is conspicuous in the early writings and in the *Phenomenology*. Metaphors are crucial to his philosophical rhetoric because they so obligingly break down at the right times. This is crucial in the indirect move to wean the reader from unreflective reliance upon picture-thinking and metaphor. So the use of metaphor, which will not do in the end to represent the Absolute, is crucial to convince the reader to recollect the whole every time a metaphor starts to take over. Metaphor is used to convince the reader to abandon metaphor and set off on Hegel's quest for a "scientific" philosophy.

Ironically, Hegel's metaphors, including the owl, serve their formative function long after they have been dispensed with in thought and their limitations revealed. Without the metaphors it would be hard to discern the overall pattern of Hegel's perlocutionary argument. Hegel's tropes play a definite role in his project to win the audience over to his perspective and his approach to the problems of philosophy. The owl of Minerva reminds us of the historical nature of Hegel's understanding of philosophical truth as a whole. His philosophical rhetoric argues in an indirect and perlocutionary fashion toward that same understanding.

One of the main questions of this book has been how to read and interpret philosophical writings. We have seen that it is in large measure left up to the reader and cannot be engineered by the machinations of the writer or user of the writing. This means that philosophical writings are ripe for a deconstructive reading. We can detect the cross-rhetorics which undercut the main line of the philosophical rhetoric of the writing. An author or writing cannot

139

compel a response from the audience. The use of force is not an option, for though the lips may give assent, the mind may not. Not compulsion, but persuasion, is the key in which philosophy is carried on. The use of tropical language in philosophy, which is only beginning to be understood, is part and parcel of the indirect means of persuasion which philosophical writings display.

Chapter Five

PHILOSOPHICAL RHETORIC

We are now in a position to describe and evaluate the concept of philosophical rhetoric. It enables us to see philosophy and rhetoric stand together inseparably in a dynamic and unstable equilibrium. From traditional rhetoric the philosophical takes the concepts of persuasion and influence; from philosophy, the concept of an independent truth. But whereas traditional rhetoric is mainly instrumental, philosophical rhetoric is not, or not directly so. Its aim is to persuade someone of a truth that is indifferent to how it is used or whether it is recognized as such. It is part of the effort made in philosophy to understand the world and our place within it, for philosophical understanding is not simply a matter of intellection but also of orientation in the world. This orientation can come only from the practitioner. The author of the writing and the writing itself can do no more than make suggestions, drop hints, stimulate the imagination and the memory, and in general move the audience as a whole to a different standpoint and attitude in which the doing of philosophy makes sense.

Philosophical rhetoric promotes a truth. Even if what comes to light is the untruth of previous truth, that is now a truth for us. For example, the sharp critique of the truth of *logos* which we find in the writings of Kierkegaard, Nietzsche, and Heidegger are at the same time promotions of a truth which is no longer thought abstractly in terms of *logos* or reason. We are to choose to will one thing, create values, and await the coming of Being. Truth is subjective. Truth is a dead metaphor. Truth is a not-forgetting. The writings of each thinker point to a truth, though perhaps not a truth which can be expressed in straightforward philosophical prose. In that sense these writers and writings, with the possible exception of Kierkegaard, break with the "logocentric" philosophical rhetoric which pervades many of the central texts of philosophy.

It is as paradoxical to hold that there is no such thing as truth as we ordinarily conceive of it as it is to support the skeptical position with arguments. It is as paradoxical as the relativist principle that the truth of any theory depends upon the assent given to it by the audience. Is the truth of the principle itself similarly so dependent? If the relativist principle is itself relative to assent, then it is false. But if it is not, then it is also false, for it would then be a proper principle and not subject to the whims of the audience. The whole point of a principle is that it should transcend the assent or dissent of the individuals who wrangle over it. Principles are universal and connect the solitary thinker to the public world of discourse. A thorough relativist must remain silent. To say anything at all is already to presuppose and utilize a *logos*. We may succeed in decentering *logos* but we will never be rid of it.

Philosophical writing takes place in a context of persuasion to the truth. We, the audience, are to be persuaded that such and such a view or thesis is true. But we cannot be persuaded directly. Persuasion is a species of perlocutionary action. The devices and tropes we have uncovered in a sampling of philosophical writings are just a few of the indirect means which the philosopher has at his or her disposal to bring about effects essential to the aim of philosophical persuasion to truth. As far as I can see, there are no samples of philosophical writing which do not display one or other device or trope as part of a rhetorical and yet philosophical strategy of persuasion. I cannot imagine a world in which the practice of what we call "philosophy" continues outside the uncertain, polemical, and competitive, historical field of institutionally based philosophical discourse. The conditions of philosophical production remain the ones which have brought the figure of the "professional philosopher" to the historical stage in the first place.

This is not the time to begin a new work on the history of "professional philosophy," but clearly it is a history which can be and is being written.[1] It is naïve to think that the institutionalization of philosophy teaching has had no effect on what philosophy is and what it is to *do* philosophy. In this wider context the polemical and rhetorical dimensions of philosophical writing begin

142

to show up like the gradual appearance of a picture on a roll of film. Take away the uncertain rhetorical context in which philosophy is written, read, and taught, and it is difficult to see the point of anyone writing or reading it.

In such a world argument is superfluous. Truth is luminous, its very statement compels acceptance and yet transcends both statement and belief. Spinoza comes very close to arguing a truth like this. Here we have a man who gives up everything to live a life of "plain living and high thinking." He writes philosophy and he does not write it for public consumption. Yet he engages with the great issues of the day, takes stands on them, and evolves his own theory in opposition to others. He writes persuasively, though only to a small group of friends. If we look closely we can find traces of Spinoza's philosophical rhetoric. Nevertheless, his philosophy is so hermetic and self-enclosed, so based on definitions and logic that it is easy to pass over his rhetoric and fail to see it altogether. And this is exactly the effect of his philosophical rhetoric: to make us forget it and see things *sub specie aeternitatis*.

Even someone as indifferent to the normal channels of rhetoric as Spinoza must provide his own if he is to write at all. Spinoza's is a philosophical plain style which hides itself so as to seem transparent. We have seen this tactic before and it seems to be one of the dominant, if not the dominant, rhetorical modes of philosophical writing. To discover Spinoza's philosophical rhetoric we should look to the margins of his texts. It is ironic that it is in the notes to his *Ethics* that Spinoza is most accommodating to the reader. In these asides Spinoza provides us with what images and metaphors he deems appropriate for the study of his philosophy. He does want us to understand what he is saying, and he is willing to use indirect techniques if he has to.

Spinoza actually employs a very powerful philosophical rhetoric which will not give way to extraneous display. He has one great truth, and among the conditions of attaining it are many extraordinary perlocutionary effects which must be brought about by the audience. In the *Essay on the Improvement of the Understanding*[2] Spinoza makes it clear that to grasp the great truth his writing points to, it is necessary to give up all the things which the world admires and respects. Like an ascetic Aristotle, Spinoza would have us give up looking for happiness in material things, in position, wealth, or fame. We should look for it somewhere else, in an intellectual love of God. Spinoza's truth eludes those who are not willing to part with the comforts of a "fallen life."

Despite his anti-rhetorical style then, Spinoza has high hopes, perhaps exaggerated hopes, for the effectiveness of philosophical argument to change people's lives. The revolution in our thoughts, perceptions, and feelings which Spinoza wants to bring about is part of the process by which we are to grasp the truth of what he is trying to persuade us. The two go together and are aspects of the same process. Surely, for Spinoza, that is the way it should be.

Spinoza seems to be writing for God or nature, but he must also write for us. And as long as he has a truth to impart, he must take care to impart it in such a way that the audience can take it in and act upon it. This audience is restricted to those who are already committed to using reason to solve practical and intellectual problems. Spinoza's philosophical rhetoric is designed to put some backbone into this commitment. He wants us to proceed without fear wherever reason may lead us and to grasp its conclusions with our whole being.

Despite the passion which animates Spinoza's philosophy, its expression is far from tropical. His style is arctic. On the surface at least, Spinoza takes his stand with the "cool" philosophers who value straightforward prose which is as clear as possible.[3] He resorts to indirection only when it is necessary to move the reader toward comprehension. He makes few allowances for the weaknesses of his audience. We have seen, however, that philosophical rhetoric comes in all shapes and sizes, and not all philosophers are "cool."

By contrast, "hot" philosophers like Kierkegaard and Nietzsche make abundant use of the means of indirection in language. Indirect techniques of communication are central to their philosophical rhetorics. Both are convinced that it is impossible to state a philosophical truth of any interest in straightforward transparent prose. The attempt to do so is doomed from the start. The "hot" philosophers disrupt the orderly consumption of philosophical material by placing question marks around the whole endeavor. They are full of tricks, imaginative, speculative, and often lacking in proper order.

Philosophers with a "hot" philosophical rhetoric are mavericks. Those with a "cool" one are more likely to be team players. This is perhaps the main reason why "hot" philosophers tend to find themselves at odds with academic institutions. Nor are they encouraged by that rite of passage called the doctorate of philosophy. Institutional life demands compromise and cooperation. The goal is to contribute to research undertaken and validated in common with one's peers. Since the "hot" philosopher does not fit in, he or she will likely have trouble playing the cooperative academic game.

An interesting example of this phenomenon is the changing placement of Wittgenstein's writings in the canon of philosophy. The trouble with Wittgenstein, and especially the later Wittgenstein, is that he is a "hot" philosopher taken to be "cool." A whole generation of philosophers were taught that Wittgenstein is a team player, and that we can carry on developing his work cooperatively. Wittgenstein's writings, and those which accumulated around them, became a standard example of what "doing philosophy" is like.

However, this runs counter to a mainstream of Wittgenstein's philosophical rhetoric. In the *Philosophical Investigations*, Wittgenstein makes it abundantly clear that he is not looking for disciples.[4] He is not proposing a "philosophy" to put alongside the others. He wants us to take another look around, but it is we who must look; Wittgenstein can only point the way. In the *Investigations* his writing is dialogical, highly metaphorical, and indirect in its effects. He is talking to the unpersuaded, and they must be so orientated that the truth will become clear to them. This is not a truth which can be stated directly. Truth, as Wittgenstein might say, cannot be stated but is rather shown or revealed in and by what we say.

As we become more aware of the anomalous nature of Wittgenstein's philosophical rhetoric, we can understand why his old dominance in the analytic tradition has faded from philosophical discussion. It took a generation to realize that philosophy cannot live on Wittgenstein alone. It is much easier to work with someone like St Thomas Aquinas or another of the great systematizers. It is harder to keep a Wittgenstein industry operating. His philosophical rhetoric will not support it. His writing is too highly self-conscious to be assimilated in any straightforward way. That makes him very difficult to teach. Wittgenstein reminds us that he is a philosopher and writes philosophy because of an inner compulsion, not because he wants or particularly likes to. Nothing is there about fitting into an orderly philosophical debate.

For a number of years Wittgenstein was made to fit into regular philosophy curricula. He figures there still, but not comfortably. It is impossible to translate Wittgenstein's philosophy into plain prose and capture the perlocutionary argument of his writings. His writing contains the indirect means for shifting us from thinking in a straightforward discursive fashion to one which is more observant and questioning. Like the metaphors which he so copiously uses, Wittgenstein's writing is incomplete and requires the participation of the reader in the investigations.

I have argued that there is no way that the perlocutionary effect of philosophical writing can be fully controlled. It cannot be controlled by the author and it cannot be controlled by someone using the author's writings. The rhetorical channels through which the arguments run flow in more than one direction. Cross-channels break up the orderly flow. At most the dominant rhetorical channels provide an invitation to read and interpret the text in favored ways. Philosophical writing can be at cross purposes with its own offical line. We saw that clearly in the case of A.J. Ayer's early book.[5]

This is not the place to enter a detailed study of indirection in Wittgenstein's writings but there is one tension in them which deserves notice. To summarize it crudely, he argues that the meanings of words comes from their use in a language. They are not some rarefied species of mental entity floating around in people's heads. On the contrary, to say that meaning is rooted in use is to point to the host of practices and institutions which give life to language. If a linguistic community supports a use of words through its practices and institutions, then those words have meaning. It is not for us to reform language and make it better. Language functions quite well as it is.

Who are philosophers to criticize language use that has a home in the practices of life? Philosophical language is language gone on holiday. It is a Rube-Goldberg contraption, all wheels and levers and pulleys which move but do no work. Where, out in the world of civil life, do we hear the kind of language that philosophers speak? Nowhere. Who can understand the philosopher's esoteric and technical vocabulary? Very few. Philosophical prose is cut off from the ordinary use of words. The result is bewitchment and captivity. We wander about in an atmosphere of airy abstractions unaware of its emptiness. Wittgenstein's use of indirect means of persuasion fills that emptiness with metaphors, stories, images, all the creations of a lively imagination. We stop looking for substance and essence, epistemological foundations, straightforward metaphysical truth, and many standard topics of a modern philosophy syllabus. The old ways of talking lack the self-understanding which Wittgenstein promotes.

But do they? There is another strand in Wittgenstein's philosophical rhetoric which ignores the fact that philosophical talk and writing are themselves rooted in practices and institutions. Philosophers are human, after all. They do not speak in a total vacuum, though it might seem that way at times. For centuries philosophers have been speaking an esoteric and technical language, but they have been speaking it. Hence, it follows that philosophical vocabularies have a perfect semantic pedigree. We look to their use and we catch on to the rules. Pretty soon we are speaking the language.

It is ironic that Wittgenstein fails to show as much toleration for philosophical language as he does for religious language. Words and sentences which have no literal meaning are allowed significance in the context of the lives of people who use religious language to express themselves. We can make sense of the last judgment if we can conceive of a life in which belief in it makes a difference.[6] In such a life the use of last judgment language is meaningful. Questions of verification and truth value fall by the wayside.

How is philosophical language different from religious language in this respect? It is a specialized and esoteric language which can be learned like any other. There are rules for the use of concepts. We are able to correct students when they make mistakes and corroborate correct uses. We can give up the language of substance and attribute, body and mind, of foundations in epistemology and so on. But if we do, it will be the effect of a perlocutionary argument and not an illocutionary one. It remains possible to speak the old language of substance and attribute. The language-games which support the use of these words are still in place. For example, when we talk about Aristotle's metaphysics, we still expect to hear the language of substance (*ousia*); when we talk about Descartes" metaphysics, we expect the language of mind and body.

There is no direct argument to show the meaninglessness of philosophical language. Wittgenstein uses a battery of indirect arguments to persuade us of his position, but it is for us to be convinced. Recent developments in post-Wittgensteinian Anglo-American philosophy suggest a return to questions and methods of an earlier era. And very recently there has been a resurgence of interest in Wittgenstein as the problematic nature of philosophy once more calls attention to itself through deconstruction. From this perspective Wittgenstein's philosophical rhetoric is appealing. The "hot" side of Wittgenstein is exploited. The interest is in Wittgenstein the maverick and the loner, not in Wittgenstein the team player.

Wittgenstein eschews the grand theory. He wants us to look and see the differences beween things. We are not to generalize too quickly. Let us not impose our views upon a recalcitrant world but note its complexities. Let us open ourselves to the possibility of gaining some real insight. Though he does not preach it, Wittgenstein practices a kind of deconstructive thought. The connection between Wittgenstein and recent French philosophy and theory has become a topic of its own. The French theoreticians are "hot" at the moment, and the "hot" side of Wittgenstein is discovered or rediscovered.[7]

Wittgenstein resists the attempt to assimilate his "thought" into a standard philosophical education. The demands of teaching and publishing push him off center-stage where he never sat well in the first place. The popularity of Wittgenstein's philosophical rhetoric has had its ups and downs and has had them in different ways. The Wittgenstein discovered by the French is hardly the Wittgenstein which appealed to the first-generation Wittgenstein-ians. What had the appeal in that case was not his potential for disrupting "logocentric" thought but his discussion of rules and logical grammar. He was harnessed to the cart of "conceptual analysis" as well as he could be and made to perform yeoman duty in the service of a collective institutional practice.

In this story the French have responded to a different Wittgenstein, one who fits more with their own ideas. There is no right or wrong here because we are simply describing the different perlocutionary effects his writings have produced. They have moved audiences in different directions relative to the complex historical situation in which they find themselves. It is this relativism which gives rise to the impressions of changing philosophical fashions. Writers and writings famous in their day have faded away. The same which languished in obscurity have found prominent discussion in the debates of later times. Alexander's *Space, Time and Deity*[8] is an example of the former, Kierkegaard's *Concluding Unscientific Postscript*[9] of the latter.

Nietzsche has come into sudden vogue. No one much reads Bergson any more. Sartre is dead. Vico is coming up on the outside.[10] We could do market research and come up with a philosophical top ten for the year. Sociological investigation will discover the popularity of different flavors of philosophical rhetoric.

However, the popularity of a philosophical rhetoric, like that of logical positivism for example, is contingent upon a number of factors beyond the control of any piece of philosophical writing. Furthermore, its popularity at any given time may have little to do with the philosophical rhetoric itself. The writings of Plato have had the effect of getting people to strive to attain complete philosophical systems. They have also had the effect of getting people to give up all systematizing. On the latter view, Plato's writings constitute the tragedy of philosophy, the impossibility of its project to attain a metaphysical truth. On the former view, his writings, though not perfect, point in the direction thought must take toward clarity and reason. The same writings have different effects in different contexts, and what determines the effects they produce is a very complex situation in which the audience plays a crucial part.

Fashions in philosophy, like fashions in clothes and music, are made by those who read the texts and buy the clothes and music. What this shows is that the popular items are producing effects in significant numbers of people. In the case of philosophy the books which everyone reads at any given time are the ones which, at that time, produce the sharpest reactions. Whether that has anything to do with the actual philosophical rhetoric in play is another question.

In the case of Wittgenstein it is fairly clear that during the time of his ascendancy, features of his philosophical rhetoric were either ignored or shunted to the margins. However, these are just the

features of Wittgenstein's philosophical rhetoric which are emphasized by the French incorporation of his work. Philosophical
writing has this in common with poetry, that the writing in
question is incomplete as it stands and requires completion by the
audience. It is a matter of audience response how, or if, that
completion comes to be.

In philosophical writing much can be done to predispose the
audience to attend to and perhaps accept the given line of
argument and its concomitant attitudes. This is the job of those
rhetorical devices and tropes which have figured in the philosophical writings studied in this book. In many cases it is quite clear
that the philosophical rhetoric concerned invites closure. The story
has a conclusion and we are invited to accept it. In other writings,
the "hot" ones, we are invited to keep the questions open and not
fix upon a canonical interpretation. These seem to be two of the
main styles of philosophical rhetoric and they exist in tension and
in the partial negation of each other.

One of the main differences lies in the use which is made of the
rhetorical and poetic resources of language. The plain cool style
and the hot tropical style diverge sharply on this point. The plain
style is wary of rhetoric and poetry; the tropical style revels in
them. A plain-style philosophical rhetoric works against speculation and flights of philosophical fancy. A tropical style encourages
the use of the imagination, tries to stretch the audience's horizons.
The plain style is suited to universities and the ongoing research of
our institutions of higher education. The tropical style provides the
strategies and tactics to negate the sober deliberations of the
professionals.

The trouble with tropical philosophy writing is that it is non-
transferable. The tropical philosophers are outsiders one and all.
Each remains stubbornly non-assimilable. They are not team
players and never can be. It would seem, therefore, that philosophy
as we know it and practice it cannot subsist on a diet of outsiders
alone. Outsiders do not exist with no inside to be outside of. The
communal, institutional setting of philosophical writing, reading,
and talking must already exist for the outsider texts to disrupt
them.

The tropical style in philosophy is one of heightened self-
awareness. In it we find those distancing techniques which allow
and invite the audience to perform a radical reflection upon itself.

The plain style, for the most part, does not. One of the interesting things about Locke's writing, for example, is how willing it is to go along with good common sense.[11] It is not a highly self-reflexive writing. Whether in politics or epistemology, Locke simply addresses himself to a rational, educated audience and asks its members to examine within themselves whether he is right. Common sense carries the day and we do not allow ourselves to go off chasing rainbows. Locke wants to make things as easy as possible for the reader. He sets out his arguments in a straightforward fashion and draws his morals the same way. Someone with a very literal cast of mind will find Locke intelligible, if not wholly persuasive.

The same cannot be said for the more indirect philosophical writing. The demands upon the audience are much greater. Not as many assumptions are made about the proper way to proceed. Faced with the writings of figures such as Kierkegaard and Nietzsche, the reader is thrown on his or her own devices to make what can be made of them. For someone with a literal cast of mind, their writings can very well appear merely paradoxical or wrong-headed. The philosophical rhetoric of both sides work on audiences with a certain intellectual orientation already in place. Only when the reader is unsure can the philosophical rhetoric of an unfamiliar position begin to work.

Tropical texts tend to shake up their audiences more than those of the plain style. A tropical philosophical rhetoric is working toward a truth which cannot be expressed directly. The plain road to truth is undermined. The rhetorical and poetic devices of indirect philosophical writings serve to disorient the audience long enough to allow a different orientation to emerge.

Philosophical writings have their own truth rhetoric. In the coolest plain style we still expect to find a pared-down use of rhetorical and poetic devices. We expect a perlocutionary argument to the effect that the efficient use of language in communication is transparent. On the other hand, even in the "hottest" philosophical writing, we find recognizable philosophical arguments. In any event we are still able to talk about good and bad arguments and their significance in the text.

Philosophical writing is a mix of direct and indirect modes of address. The emphasis may vary from text to text, but both are contained in each. One of the main purposes of this study has been to bring out just how pervasive indirection is in the writings of philosophy. Truth must be made persuasive to declare itself to others. Without a philosophical rhetoric of truth, philosophical investigation or conversation remains without motivation.

I would like to conclude this book with one more point of comparison between plain and tropical philosophy. It centers on the concept of ingenuity. As a term of ancient rhetoric ingenuity is the ability to come up with arguments. It is the ability to make surprising or novel connections. Later, Giambattista Vico made ingenuity central to his imaginative reliving of the founding and development of human political, scientific, philosophical, religious, economic, and aesthetic institutions and practices. All of these "inventions of human being" arise from the "faculty of bringing together things that are disparate and widely separated."[12]

According to Vico it was by making the connection between, for example, thunder in the sky and Jove's body that the first people began to recognize themselves as a people. Thunder became the voice of a god by analogy with their own bodies and the sounds they emitted. They recognized their dependence upon an external power by seeing how weak their voices were in comparison to the thunder of Zeus. This is an invention of the human mind which tries to grasp its own nature and place in the scheme of things. It is through metaphor, an unlikely relation of wildly different objects, that human beings begin to conceptualize and understand themselves.

Conceptualization and self-understanding or self-awareness begin in metaphor, but do not end there. Once we have a metaphor in our imagination it can work to produce questions, problems, and exciting avenues of investigation. Whether a metaphor remains suggestive or dies, by itself it never solves the problems or answers the questions which it suggests, that must be left to a reflective audience. The response of this audience is what we have come to call philosophy.

Vico is right to argue that thought starts with poetry and ends with philosophy. Philosophy is the death of poetry, but poetry is the heart of philosophy and lives again there. The images and tropes which make a place for themselves in memory become a resource of thought. The power of a philosophical metaphor, irony, or paradox is the power to produce perlocutionary effects. They induce the audience to feel the invitation to think incompatible thoughts as if they had connections between them. Imagination is needed to bring color and detail to philosophical abstractions.

What the techniques of indirection in philosophical writing ask of the audience is ingenuity. Tropes, metaphors, and the rest invite the audience to exercise its ingenuity in filling them out and making sense of them. Tropical philosophy stimulates the inventiveness of the audience. Whether such philosophical writing succeeds or not will be a perlocutionary effect on a particular audience.

Rhetoric operates in a public arena in which the events to come cannot be foreseen. A decision is asked for about some projected future or alternative futures which are conditioned by the decision itself. The future, though it does not yet exist, is as much made by the decisions and actions of human beings as by factors beyond their control. This is particularly true in areas in which long-term human practices have effects far beyond their immediate impact.

A good example is the effect that human practices are having on the long-term prospects for the survival of mammals on this planet. Public policy in this area is hedged with uncertainty. Stands are taken on the bases of probabilities and produce effects outside anyone's immediate control. Yet those effects will be in large part the result of those "probable" decisions. Many of the things that human beings are doing on this planet have untold side-effects, some of which may be irreversible. Yet we still have to act on the most plausible beliefs we can muster and hope for the best.

The debates about the environment and how best to protect it are intensely practical and urgent. At issue is the problem of how we are going to shape our environment with an eye to our own survival as a species. What we say actually shapes that environment by putting into motion the projects which will change the world as we find it. The power which technical prowess promised in the seventeenth century has come into our collective hands. We must use it. It is out of the question not to use it, since its effects have already changed the face of the world. It is a real question now whether we want to turn rivers around, tunnel through mountains, dump our waste into the sea, conduct atomic tests, continue to use fertilizers and pesticides, leave the lead in gasoline . . . the list is practically endless. In these cases we act in ignorance of all the effects our actions have, but we know that the decisions we make play a role in the outcome.

What I want to draw attention to in this example is the way that the world adapts itself to our words as much as our words adapt themselves to the world. To act is to move to change the world in a certain way. If we describe to the best of our knowledge the effects of a nuclear winter upon the quality of mammalian life, we are hoping that our words fit the world, that they are true of it. If they do, and we are convincing, then the fact that a nuclear winter would follow the outbreak of global nuclear war fits nicely with the practical project of making the world safe from nuclear war. For example, by forming the policy of eliminating all nuclear weapons, we hope to make the world take the shape our policy prescribes. Certainly, the world existed without nuclear weapons before 1945, and it could do so again. There is nothing in the nature of things which prevents it except ourselves.

The point is that a future state is projected and what comes to be is partly shaped by that project. Often the effects far exceed or even undercut the intentions of the promulgators of policy. Sartre gives a good example of this in the story of how the conscious projects of the Girondists in the French revolution turned out badly for them.[13] Their projects had untoward effects which passed beyond their control. Yet those very same projects helped to bring about those effects, and the Girondists did have an effect on the course of events leading to their own demise.

Philosophical writing is analogous. Philosophy as a way of discussion and argument has a past and has a future. Though it may take on timeless questions, it does so in a "timely" environment. There is nothing eternal about philosophy as now practiced in the universities of the west. Its future is as assured as next year's funding. The breakup of the university system would have a severe effect on the transmission lines of history and thought but it is not impossible to contemplate such a state of affairs.

Whatever its topic, philosophical writing is addressed to an audience and designed with the intention and hope of making some impression there. The sober, plain style of philosophical rhetoric works calmly to clear the head of a presumably confused audience. The role of ingenuity is played down and the role of method is played up. Method befits a discursive philosophy, for it can be set out and clearly stated. Ingenuity does not work like that. There is no way to teach someone to be ingenious; rather, ingenuity can be encouraged or discouraged.

The strong claim for ingenuity is that it actually creates the world in which we live and of which we have experience. Thought is empty without a strong metaphor to drive it on. When the metaphor dies, the philosophy around it becomes isolated and ultimately vacuous. A hot style burns itself out in unintelligibility and a cold one becomes completely abstract, esoteric, and finally boring.

On this view we construct the world imaginatively out of metaphors and then proceed to understand the world in those terms for as long as they hold up. This poetic construct we call the world maintains its protean character through all transformations. No totalizing spirit adds everything up. Yet it is through the rise and collapse of metaphors that we can trace the progress of the failure of philosophical writing to deliver all that it promises.

The tropical philosophers make extensive comment upon the failure of traditional philosophy to capture the essence of Being, the foundations of knowledge, morality, and the other "perennial" questions of philosophy. They are ingenious philosophers who call heavily upon the ingenuity, not to say the patience, of the audience. Language fails to express what can be only pointed to. The poverty of language forces us to use our ingenuity in forging tropes to suit our needs.

As both the world and our perception of it change through time, new objects come upon the horizon, new relations are entered into, new analogies and metaphors help us to orientate ourselves toward a changing situation. We try to find a way to express something which cannot be expressed directly, something unfamiliar, by analogy with something we already understand. Or by relating the familiar world to something strange and unfamiliar, we indirectly invite a radical reflection upon that familiar world. It works both ways. In either case the effects depend upon a telling deformation of language. Whether and how the point will be taken, or the image take root in memory, depends on the audience picking up the cues in the text.

Ingenuity is the ability to pick up cues and follow signs. In philosophy that means making connections between concepts which do not follow some well-marked trail. There is no method of indirect writing which can be followed in a step-by-step fashion. As Plato said of the poets, they have the grace to speak of different things to different people. Only those with the ingenuity to do so will be able to extract the hidden meanings of the poets. The trouble with Protagoras, we recall, is that he comes right out and publicizes a technique which can be acquired both by those who have judgment and understanding and by those who do not.[14]

Tropical writing in philosophy relies heavily upon ingenuity for the production of striking metaphors, synecdoches, analogies, ironies, paradoxes, and the rest. The effectiveness of the tropes, in turn, relies equally heavily upon the ingenuity of the audience. The whole enterprise is a risky and uncertain business. The ability to see connections where none existed before, to surmount difficulties as they appear without appeal to method, is a very uncertain one. It is not very reliable to depend upon the audience's ingenuity to follow an intuitive series of thoughts. The whole business of tropical philosophy remains problematic.

Against the strong claim for ingenuity in philosophical writing are the arguments we have already rehearsed questioning the use of metaphor and other tropes in philosophical writing. Ingenuity is for writings with a hot philosophical rhetoric. Cooler heads will prefer a more unobtrusive philosophical rhetoric aimed at truths which can be expressed and argued in a more pedestrian and straightforward fashion, though even here the techniques of indirection in philosophical writing cannot be relinquished entirely. An over-zealous criticism of ingenuity in philosophical deliberations tends to overlook this fact.

On the other hand, an over-zealous embrace of ingenuity can have its own dire effects upon our thinking. The action of ingenuity is to break through limits by making novel connections between things. To do so without restraint leads to the production of writings with a baroque or mannerist philosophical rhetoric, a kind of wit which leaves one hungering for something a bit more substantial. The exhilaration which comes from breaking limits becomes self-stultifying if taken as an end in itself. There are limits to our capacity to create a world which is as much the way we find it as the way we make it. We are as much products of our world as producers of it. A consideration of philosophical rhetoric constantly reminds us of both sides and of the dialectical tension in which they exist.

We have at our disposal as speakers of a language and members of a species and culture the means for both direct and indirect communication and expression. Actual utterances and writings contain both. To forget one in pursuit of the other is to lose touch with the complex situation which informs the rhetorical context of philosophical writing and speaking and the place of straight-forward argument within it.

Whether predominantly hot or cold, philosophical writings display their own rhetoric though they do not state it. It is important that we acquire the means to spot the workings of philosophical rhetoric in philosophical writings. To ignore it and rest content with a simple distinction between philosophy and rhetoric does not do justice to the contentious field of philosophical endeavor. It is no longer possible to ignore the indirect arguments and invited perlocutionary effects which philosophical writing produces. Whether the style is hot or cold, we can look for the perlocutionary arguments which inform philosophical productions.

This does not mean, as I argued in Chapter 3, that philosophical investigation and argument become impossible or fraudulent. What it does mean is that to be in a position to appreciate the argument, the audience must already have been brought around to a perspective in which both the questions asked and the answers proposed take on a cogency they would not otherwise possess. Indirection in philosophical writing has everything to do with creating the setting in which the arguments for various theses are put forward. An appeal is made to the audience to take up a position and then to work through its implications. The audience comes to recognize its value or even truth by working through those implications. A successful philosophical rhetoric has this primary effect: it gets a hearing for the position put forward. Without acceptance of some basis for discussion, philosophical investigation cannot proceed.

An anecdote will illustrate this point. I attended a Kant class as an undergraduate in which we were to cover the Analytic – space, time, the categories, and so on. Kant's transcendental question is "How is empirical knowledge possible?"[15] It presupposes that we do in fact possess empirical knowledge. A student in the class, who shall remain nameless, simply would not accept this. He remained at the level of one of Hegel's skeptics who cry out "no" when someone says "yes" and vice versa.[16] You can imagine how vexing this was to the teacher. A determined skeptic is always able to question the spoken and unspoken assumptions of any philoso-phical theory. However, if that is done, it is impossible to make progress with Kant or any other philosopher. Both Kant's philosophical rhetoric and the teacher's best efforts failed to bring this student around. The result was that in a whole semester we never left the Aesthetic.

Austin speaks of "securing uptake" in the audience of an illocutionary act.[17] Something analogous occurs in philosophical writing at the level of the perlocutionary act. The writer's and the writing's philosophical rhetoric must ensure that the audience's attention is secured and interest aroused. The audience must be motivated to want to understand what is being said. Otherwise the whole argument falls on deaf ears and is wasted. The first thing a piece of philosophical writing must do is secure uptake, not merely in the sense of preparing the audience to understand a straight-forward communication, but in the sense of persuading it to adopt the appropriate orientation and attitude to what is written.

The perlocutionary effects of philosophical writing are largely in the hands of the audience. The mainline philosophical rhetoric of a text suggests its own authorized perspective, but we do not have to read it that way. We can read a philosophical text against the grain. We can look to margins of the text to help us with our own endeavors.

This book has been an attempt to outline a concept of philosophical rhetoric and to sensitize ourselves to its functioning in philosophical writing. If nothing else, the concept suggests a wide area of further research. Perhaps more important, it encourages a thoroughgoing reflectiveness on the part of those who produce philosophical writings, making them aware of their own philosophical rhetoric and the techniques of indirection they employ.

NOTES

PREFACE

1 See Bibliography.
2 Willard Van Orman Quine, *Word and Object*, Cambridge, MA, MIT Press, 1960.
3 J. Derrida, *Margins of Philosophy*, Hassocks, Harvester, 1982.
4 J.L. Austin, *Philosophical Papers*, ed. J.O. Urmson and G.J. Warnock, Oxford, Clarendon Press 1961; *How to Do Things with Words*, ed. J.O. Urmson and Marina Sbisa, Oxford, Oxford University Press, 1986.
5 A.J. Ayer, *Language, Truth and Logic*, Harmondsworth, Pelican Books, 1972.
6 G.W.F. Hegel, *The Phenomenology of Spirit*, trans. A.V. Miller, Oxford, Oxford University Press, 1979.
7 Immanual Kant, *Critique of Pure Reason*, trans. N. Kemp Smith, London, Macmillan, 1973, pp. 210–11, 450ff.

CHAPTER 1 INTRODUCTION: PHILOSOPHY AND RHETORIC

1 See Bibliography.
2 Michel Foucault, *Power/Knowledge: Selected Interviews and Other Writings 1972–1977*, ed. Peter Gordon, New York, Pantheon Books, 1980; see especially pp. 109–34.
3 Plato, *Gorgias*, 521e33–522a6.
4 ibid., 465a1–7.
5 "The world turned upside-down: estrangement in the philosophy of Plato", forthcoming, *Journal of Literary Semantics*.
6 Plato, *Gorgias*, 484c4–486d.
7 Plato, *Republic*, book VII.
8 Aristotle, *Rhetoric*, 1357a24 ff.
9 Aristotle, *Nichomachean Ethics*, 1103b27 ff.
10 Cicero, *De Oratore* 3.16.60–61, trans. E.W. Sutton and H. Rickham, London and New York, Loeb Edition.

11 See Walter J. Ong, *Rhetoric, Romance and Technology*, Ithaca, NY, and London, Cornell University Press, 1971, passim.
12 See Jonathan Rée, "Philosophy as an academic discipline," *Studies in Higher Education*, III (1), March 1978.

CHAPTER 2 CASE STUDIES: SCHOPENHAUER, KIERKEGAARD, WITTGENSTEIN AND NIETZSCHE

1 The true death is something like nirvana. It is the point at which it is no longer necessary to keep coming back for more lives.
2 Arthur Schopenhauer, *The World as Will and Representation*, trans. E.F.J. Payne, New York, Dover Publications, 1969.
3 ibid., vol. II, p. 209.
4 ibid., p. 207.
5 ibid., vol. I, p. 104.
6 ibid.
7 ibid., vol. II, p. 639.
8 Søren Kierkegaard, *The Concluding Unscientific Postscript*, trans. David F. Swenson and Walter Lowrie, Princeton, NJ, Princeton University Press, 1968.
9 Ludwig Wittgenstein, *Philosophical Investigations*, trans. G.E.M. Anscombe, New York, Macmillan, 1965.
10 Ludwig Wittgenstein, *Tractatus Logico-Philosophicus*, New York and London, Routledge & Kegan Paul, 1961.
11 For an interesting discussion of Nietzsche's rhetorical strategy see Paul De Man's *Allegories of Reading*, New Haven, CT, and London, Yale University Press, 1979, especially Chapters 5 and 6 of Part I. He makes the point that Nietzsche's writing disrupts and deconstructs the forms of traditional philosophical investigation.
12 Friedrich Nietzsche, *The Will to Power*, trans. Walter Kaufmann and R.J. Hollingdale, New York, Random House, 1968, pp. 35–6.
13 Saul Kripke, *Naming and Necessity*, Oxford, Blackwell, 1980.
14 Wittgenstein, *Philosophical Investigations*, p. 19.
15 J.L. Austin, *How to do Things with Words*, ed. J.O. Urmson and Marina Sbisa, Oxford, Oxford University Press, 1986.
16 Wittgenstein, *Philosophical Investigations*, section 23.
17 Austin, *How to Do Things with Words*, pp. 109, 115.
18 ibid., pp. 109, 119.
19 G.E.M. Anscombe, *Intention*, Oxford, Blackwell, 1966, pp. 16f.
20 René Descartes, *Discourse on Method and Meditations*, trans. Laurence J. Lafleur, New York, Bobbs-Merrill, 1960, book I.
21 See J. Rée, *Philosophical Tales*, London, Methuen, 1987, p. 19.
22 Descartes, *Discourse on Method and Meditations*, pp. 77, 80.
23 René Descartes, *Meditations on the First Philosophy*, trans. J. Cottingham, Cambridge, Cambridge University Press, 1986, p. 14.
24 ibid. pp. 51, 55.

CHAPTER 3 INDIRECTION, PERLOCUTIONARY ACTION, AND RHETORIC

1 Richard Rorty, *Philosophy and the Mirror of Nature*, Princeton, N.J. Princeton University Press, 1977, pp. 389–94.
2 Catherine Belsey, *Critical Practice*, London, Methuen, 1980, pp. 108–9. Ms Belsey offers us a synopsis of Pierre Macherey's account of Verne's novel (Pierre Macherey, *A Theory of Literary Production*, trans. Geoffrey Wall, London, Routledge & Kegan Paul, 1978, pp. 159ff).
3 A.J. Ayer, *Language, Truth and Logic*, Harmondsworth, Pelican Books, 1952.
4 Immanuel Kant, *Critique of Pure Reason*, trans. N. Kemp Smith, London, Macmillan, 1973, pp. 25–76.
5 Ludwig Wittgenstein, *Philosophical Investigations*, trans. G.E.M. Anscombe, New York, Macmillan, 1965, p. 194.
6 Plato, *Gorgias*, 480b7-d6; 508b5–7.
7 J. Derrida, *Margins of Philosophy*, Hassocks, Harvester, 1982, pp. 1–29.
8 Sir Philip Sidney; see *Sidney: A Defence of Poetry*, ed. Jan van Dorsten, Oxford, Oxford University Press, 1975, p. 25.
9 Plato, *Republic*, 509d1–511e.
10 Plato, *Phaedrus*, 274c6–275b2.
11 Kant, *Critique*, p. 538.
12 M. Heidegger, *Being and Time*, trans. John Macquarrie and Edward Robinson, Oxford, Blackwell, 1967, pp. 21–36.
13 Wittgenstein, *Philosophical Investigations*, p. 217.
14 ibid., pp. 87, 200, 217, 326, 485.
15 Derrida, *Margins*, pp. 1–29.
16 Lewis White Beck (ed.), *Kant on History*, New York, Bobbs-Merrill, 1963, pp. 11–27.
17 Plato, *Republic*, 336–354.
18 Plato, *Theaetetus*, 152a.
19 Plato, *Gorgias*, 4626–9–462c7.
20 Plato seems to have changed his mind somewhat on this question. In the *Gorgias*, Socrates condemns rhetoric as a merely pandering to our basest desires. In the *Phaedrus*, however, he seems to grant a more positive use of rhetoric in philosophy.
21 See A. Schrift, "Language, metaphor, rhetoric: Nietzsche's deconstruction of epistemology," *Journal of the History of Philosophy* XXIII (3), July 1985, 371–95.

CHAPTER 4 TROPICAL PHILOSOPHY

1 G. Vico, *The New Science of Giambattista Vico*, trans. T.G. Bergin and M.H. Fisch, Ithaca, NY, Cornell University Press, 1961, p. 57.
2 Plato, *Republic*, books III, X.
3 Plato, *Republic*, 394ff.
4 ibid., 521cff.

5 ibid., 379a-c, 390–2, 381d.
6 I would like to acknowledge this point and this way of putting it to Dr William Macomber who first pointed out to me the unique relation in which we stand to poetry as an object of knowledge.
7 Plato, *Republic*, 379–94.
8 Plato, *Theaetetus*, 180c6-d6.
9 Plato, *Ion*, 536ff.
10 Plato, *Phaedrus*, 246al-b4, 247a4-249c4.
11 Plato, *Republic*, 621.
12 See Charles Griswold, Jr, *Self-Knowledge in Plato's Phaedrus*, New Haven, CT, and London, Yale University Press, 1986, pp. 36–44.
13 Plato, *Republic*, 508d-509a, 511b3-cl, 516b3–6, 540a3-b4.
14 ibid., book V, 451ff.
15 ibid., 518c3-dl.
16 Ludwig Wittgenstein, *Philosophical Investigations*, trans. G.E.M. Anscombe, New York, Macmillan, 1965, pp. 109, 115.
17 ibid. p. 127.
18 In oral cultures, as Walter Ong argues (*Orality and Literary*, London and New York, Methuen 1982) poetry is exclusively spoken. The introduction of writing fixes a poem in a way in which memorization and verbal repetition never can. Nevertheless, though the bard was free to improvise, it was within the framework of a widely known story. The poet would not be singing about Achilles if he did not have him sulk in his tent and avenge the death of his lover.
19 Plato, *Parmenides*, 130b1–135d8.
20 Plato, *Theaetetus*, 147a1-c7.
21 Plato, *Crito*, 49d1-e4.
22 Plato, *Gorgias*, 508e8–509a6.
23 Plato, *Republic*, 516b4–7.
24 A particularly interesting and provocative discussion of metaphor and philosophy is found in Derrida's article "White mythology" in *Margins of Philosophy* (Hassocks, Harvester, 1982). The reason I have not dealt with it explicitly is that Derrida's prose is too much like the tar baby. Touch it too hard and it sticks. I have chosen an oblique approach to Derrida to maintain momentum and avoid becoming immobilized in other debates. This is not a criticism of Derrida but a decision on my part. I crave the reader's indulgence.
25 Donald Davidson, *Inquiries into Truth and Interpretation*, Oxford, Clarendon Press, 1984, p. 245.
26 ibid., p. 246. For Max Black's views, see the editor's Introduction to Andrew Ortony (ed.), *Metaphor and Thought*, Cambridge, Cambridge University Press, 1979.
27 John Locke, *An Essay Concerning Human Understanding*, ed. Peter H. Nidditch, Oxford, Oxford University Press, 1985, Book II, Chapter I, p. 104.
28 G. Leibniz, *New Essays on Human Understanding*, trans. P. Remnant and J. Bennett, Cambridge, Cambridge University Press, 1981, Book 1, Chapter I, p. 86.

29 See Stephen Pepper, *World Hypotheses: A Study in Evidence*, Berkeley, CA, University of California Press, 1961, Chapter IX.
30 Locke, *Essay*, "Epistle to the reader," p. 10.
31 J.L. Austin, *How to Do Things with Words*, ed. J.O. Urmson and Marina Sbisa, Oxford, Oxford University Press, 1986, pp. 109, 115.
32 See Walter Ong's introduction to Petrus Ramus, *Scholae in Liberales Artes*, Hildesheim and New York, Georg Olms Verlag, 1970, pp. v-ix.
33 Aristotle, *Nicomachean Ethics*, 1094b12–15.
34 H.P. Grice, "Logic and conversation," in P. Cole and J. Morgan (eds), *Syntax and Semantics*, 3, New York and London, Academic Press, pp. 41–58.
35 David Hume, *Enquiries Concerning Human Understanding and Concerning the Principles of Morals*, Oxford, Clarendon Press, 1986, p. 63.
36 See John Searle's *Minds, Brains and Science*, Cambridge, MA, Harvard University Press, 1984.
37 Locke, *Essay*, "Epistle to the reader," p. 6.
38 Immanuel Kant, *Critique of Pure Reason*, trans. N. Kemp Smith, New York, Macmillan, 1973, p. 47.
39 G.W.F. Hegel, *Philosophy of Right*, trans. T. Knox, London, Oxford University Press, 1942, p. 13.
40 G.W.F. Hegel, *The Phenomenology of Mind*, trans. J.B. Baillie, London, Allen & Unwin, 1961, pp. 761, 789.
41 See John H. Smith, "Rhetorical polemics and the dialectic of *Kritik* in Hegel's Jena essays," *Philosophy and Rhetoric* XVIII (1), 1985, 31–58.

CHAPTER 5 PHILOSOPHICAL RHETORIC

1 See Jonathan Rée; "Philosophy as an academic discipline: the changing place of philosophy in an arts education," *Studies in Higher Education* 3, (1), 1978, 5–23.
2 B. Spinoza, *Ethics, Preceded by On the Improvement of the Understanding*, New York and London, Hafner Press, Macmillan, 1974, pp. 3–7.
3 The distinction between "hot" and "cold" philosophers came up in discussion with Prof. David Hamlyn. He remarked that teachers of philosophy could be described by these adjectives. The paradigm of a "hot" philosopher is Socrates on one end of a log and a student on the other. The paradigm of the "cooler" type is Aristotle calmly giving a lecture to a group of students.
4 Ludwig Wittgenstein, *Philosophical Investigations*, trans. G.E.M. Anscombe, New York, Macmillan, 1965.
5 A.J. Ayer, *Language, Truth and Logic*, Harmondsworth, Pelican Books, 1972.
6 Ludwig Wittgenstein, *Lectures and Conversations on Aesthetics, Psychology and Religious Belief*, ed. Cyril Barrett, Berkeley and Los Angeles, CA, University of California Press, 1983, pp. 53–64.

7 Some of the "hot" French theoreticians and Derrida, Deleuze, Foucault, and Lyotard, for example.
8 S. Alexander, *Space, Time and Diety*, London, Macmillan, 1927.
9 S. Kierkegaard, *The Concluding Unscientific Postscript*, Princeton, NJ, Princeton University Press, 1941.
10 G. Vico, *The New Science of Giambattista Vico*, trans. T.G. Bergin and M.H. Fisch, Ithaca, NY, Cornell University Press, 1961.
11 John Locke, *An Essay Concerning Human Understanding*, ed. Peter H. Nidditch, Oxford, Oxford University Press, 1985, p. 508.
12 Michael Mooney, *Vico in the Tradition of Rhetoric*, Princeton, NJ, Princeton University Press, 1958, p. 151.
13 J.-P. Sartre *Search for a Method*, trans. Hazel Barnes, New York, Vintage Books, 1968, p. 45.
14 Plato, *Theaetetus*, 152c–153d.
15 Immanuel Kant, *Prolegomena to any Future Metaphysics*, trans. P. Gary Lewis, Manchester, Manchester University Press, 1978, pp. 52–3.
16 G.W.F. Hegel, *Phenomenology of Spirit*, trans. A.V. Miller, Oxford, Oxford University Press, 1979, p. 129.
17 J.L. Austin, *How to Do Things with Words*, ed. J.O. Urmson and Marina Sbisa, Oxford, Oxford University Press, 1986.

SELECT BIBLIOGRAPHY

Included in this Select bibliography are the books which formed the background for my reflections on philosophy and rhetoric. Not all of them are mentioned explicitly but all have a bearing on the issues raised in the book. Those specifically cited in the book are included in the Notes.

Atkinson, J. (ed.), *Structures of Social Action: Studies in Conversational Analysis*, Cambridge, Cambridge University Press, 1984.

Austin, J.L., *Philosophical Papers*, ed. J.O. Urmson and G.J. Warnock, Oxford, Clarendon Press, 1961.

Baker, G. and Hacker, P., *Language, Sense and Nonsense*, Oxford, Blackwell, 1984.

Beer, J., *Narrative Conventions of Truth in the Middle Ages*, Geneva, Librairie Droz, 1981.

Belsey, C., *Critical Practice*, London and New York, Methuen, 1980.

Bennett, T., *Formalism and Marxism*, London, Methuen, 1979.

Burks, D., *Rhetoric, Philosophy and Literature: An Exploration*, West Lafayette, IN., Purdue University Press, 1978.

Butler, H.E. (ed.), *Quintilian (Vol. III): Books VII-IX*, Cambridge, MA, Harvard University Press, Loeb Classical Library, 1976.

Connors, R. (ed.), *Essays on Classical Rhetoric and Modern Discourse*, Carbondale and Edwardsville, IL, Southern Illinois University Press, 1984.

Corbett, E., *Classical Rhetoric for the Modern Student*, Oxford, Oxford University Press, 1971.

Culler, J., *Structuralist Poetics*, London, Routledge & Kegan Paul, 1975.

——, *On Deconstruction: Theory and Criticism after Structuralism*, London, Routledge & Kegan Paul, 1983.

Curran, J., "The rhetorical technique of Plato's *Phaedrus*," *Philosophy and Rhetoric* XIX (1), 1986, 66–72.

Daniel, S., "The philosophy of ingenuity: Vico on proto-philosophy," *Philosophy and Rhetoric* XVIII, (4), 1985, 236–44.

Davidson, D., *Inquiries into Truth and Interpretation*, Oxford, Clarendon Press, 1984.

Deleuze, Gilles and Felix Guattari, *Anti-Oedipus*, trans. Robert Hurley, New York, Frontis, 1977.

De Man, P., *Allegories of Reading*, New Haven, CT and London, Yale University Press, 1979.

Derrida, J., *Margins of Philosophy*, Hassocks, Harvester Press, 1982.

Descombes, V., *Modern French Philosophy*, Cambridge, Cambridge University Press, 1980.

Diem, H., *Kierkegaard: An Introduction*, Richmond, VA, John Knox Press, 1966.

Dixon, P., *Rhetoric*, London, Methuen, 1971.

Dowling, W., *Jameson, Althusser, Marx*, London, Methuen, 1984.

Erlich, V., *Russian Formalism: History-Doctrine*, New Haven, CT and London, Yale University Press, 1981.

Espy, W., *The Garden of Eloquence: A Rhetorical Bestiary*, New York, Harper & Row, 1983.

Garver, E., "Aristotle's *Rhetoric* as a work of philosophy," *Philosophy and Rhetoric*, XIX, (1), 1986, 1–22.

Gill, J., *Wittgenstein and Metaphor*, Washington, DC, University Press of America, 1981.

Griswold, C. *Self-Knowledge in Plato's Phaedrus*, New Haven, CT and London, Yale University Press, 1986.

Harwood, J. (ed.), *The Rhetorics of Thomas Hobbes and Bernard Lamy*, Carbondale and Edwardsville, IL Southern Illinois University Press, 1986.

Jameson, F., *Marxism and Form*, Princeton, NJ, Princeton University Press, 1971.

——, *The Political Unconscious*, London, Methuen, 1981.

Jordan, M., "Authority and persuasion in philosophy," *Philosophy and Rhetoric* XVIII (2), 1985, 67–86.

Harrison, B., "The truth about metaphor," *Philosophy and Literature* X (1), 1986, 38–56.

Harvey, I., "Contemporary French thought and the art of Rhetoric," *Philosophy and Rhetoric* XVIII (4), 1985, 199–216.

Hawkes, T., *Metaphor*, London, Methuen, 1972.

——, *Structuralism and Semiotics*, London, Methuen, 1977.

Heidegger, M., *Poetry, Language, Thought*, New York, Harper & Row, 1971.

Kierkegaard, Søren, *The Concluding Unscientific Postscript*, trans. David F. Swenson and Walter Lowrie, Princeton, NJ, Princeton University Press, 1968.

Knoblauch, C. and Brannon, L., *Rhetorical Traditions and the Teaching of Writing*, Upper Montclair NJ, Boynton/Cook, 1984.

Lacan, J., *Ecrits: A Selection*, New York and London, W.W. Norton, 1977.

Lecercle, J.-J., *Philosophy through the Looking-Glass*, London, Hutchinson, 1985.

Lemaire, A., *Jacques Lacan*, London, Routledge & Kegan Paul, 1977.

Levinson, S., *Pragmatics*, Cambridge, Cambridge University Press, 1983.

Lyotard, J., *The Postmodern Condition: A Report on Knowledge*, Manchester, Manchester University Press, 1984.

Macdonell, D., *Theories of Discourse: An Introduction*, Oxford, Blackwell, 1986.
Macherey, P., *A Theory of Literary Production*, London, Routledge & Kegan Paul, 1978.
Mooney, M., *Vico in the Tradition of Rhetoric*, Princeton, NJ, Princeton University Press, 1985.
Nietzsche, Friedrich, *The Will to Power*, trans. W. Kaufmann and R.J. Hollingdale, New York, Random House, 1968.
Norrick, N., "Stock similes", *Journal of Literary Semantics*, XV (1), 1986, 39–52.
Norris, C., *Deconstruction: Theory and Practice*, London, Methuen, 1982.
——, *The Contest of Faculties: Philosophy and Theory after Deconstruction*, London and New York, Methuen, 1985.
Ong, W., *Rhetoric, Romance and Technology*, Ithaca, NY and London, Cornell University Press, 1971.
Ortony, A. (ed.), *Metaphor and Thought*, Cambridge, Cambridge University Press, 1979.
Paprotte, W. and Dirven, R. (eds), *The Ubiquity of Metaphor (Current Issues in Linguistic Theory*, XXIX, Amsterdam Studies in the Theory and History of Linguistic Science), Amsterdam and Philadelphia, PA, John Benjamins Publishing Co., 1985.
Pepper, S., *World Hypotheses: A Study in Evidence*, Berkeley and Los Angeles, CA, University of California Press, 1961.
Quintilian, *On the Early Education of the Citizen-Orator*, Indianapolis, N, Bobbs-Merrill, 1965.
Rée, J., *Philosophical Tales*, London, Methuen, 1987.
Richards, I.A., *The Philosophy of Rhetoric*, London, Oxford and New York, Oxford University Press, 1964.
Schrift, A., "Language, metaphor, rhetoric: Nietzsche's deconstruction of epistemology," *Journal of the History of Philosophy*, XXIII (3), 1985, 371–95.
Seldon, R., *A Reader's Guide to Contemporary Literary Theory*, Hassocks, Harvester Press, 1985.
Shaw, D., "Nietzsche as sophist: a polemic," *International Philosophical Quarterly*, XXVI (4), 1986, 331–9.
Sherman, C., *Reading Voltaire's Contes: A Semiotics of Philosophical Narration*, Chapel Hill, NC, University of North Carolina Press, 1985.
Smith, J., "Rhetorical polemics and the dialectics of *Kritik* in Hegel's Jena essays," *Philosophy and Rhetoric*, XVIII (1), 1985, 31–58.
Sontag, F., *A Kierkegaard Handbook*, Atlanta, GA, John Knox Press, 1979.
Steiner, P., *Russian Formalism: A Metapoetics*, Ithaca, NY and London, Cornell University Press, 1984.
Sturrock, J., *Structuralism and Since: From Levi Strauss to Derrida*, Oxford, Oxford University Press, 1979.
Tagliacozzo, G. (ed.), *Giambattista Vico's Science of Humanity*, Baltimore, MD and London, Johns Hopkins University Press, 1976.
Taylor, W. (ed.), *Metaphors of Education*, London, Heinemann Educational Books, 1984.
Thulstrup, N., *Commentary on Kierkegaard's Concluding Unscientific Postscript*,

trans. R. Widenmann, Princeton, NJ, Princeton University Press, 1984.

Veit, W., "The potency of imagery – the impotence of rational language: Ernesto Grassi's contribution to modern epistemology," *Philosophy and Rhetoric*, XVII (4), 1984, 221–40.

Verene, D., *Vico's Science of Imagination*, Ithaca, NY and London, Cornell University Press, 1981.

——, *Hegel's Recollection: A Study of Images in the Phenomenology of Spirit*, Albany, NY, State University of New York Press, 1985.

Waterhouse, R., *A Heidegger Critique*, Hassocks, Harvester, 1981.

White, E., *Rhetoric in Transition: Studies in the Nature and Uses of Rhetoric*, University Park, PA and London, Pennsylvania State University Press, 1980.

INDEX